WORLD FAMOUS

# GREAT EXPLORERS

Vikas Khatri

PUSTAK MAHAL®

*Publishers*
**Pustak Mahal®**

***Administrative office and sale centre***

J-3/16 , Daryaganj, New Delhi-110002
☎ 23276539, 23272783, 23272784 • *Fax:* 011-23260518
*E-mail:* info@pustakmahal.com • *Website:* www.pustakmahal.com

***Branches***
**Bengaluru:** ☎ 080-22234025 • *Telefax:* 080-22240209
*E-mail*: pustakmahalblr@gmail.com
**Mumbai:** ☎ 022-22010941, 022-22053387
*E-mail*: unicornbooksmumbai@gmail.com



ISBN 978-81-223-1326-0

**Edition: 2018**



**Printed at: Ar Emm International, Delhi.**

# Introduction

Since the dawn of human civilization, constant need of human expansion set the army of explorers to discover new lands and new routes to travel across the unfamiliar terrain. Those early periods of exploration proved to be instrumental in the future, and they paved the way for all the future explorers that imagined strange lands just beyond horizon.

As we look back into history, the most prominent era for the explorers was without a doubt a time between 15th and 17th century, when European countries began exploring the continents of Americas. However, those discoveries would never be made without the efforts of the ancient explorers from almost 2000 years ago. Tales of the journeys of Skylax (who managed to circumvent Arabian Peninsula in 500 BC), Pytheas (who in 300 BC discovered England, Scandinavia and polar ice) and Alexander the Great (who explored the areas of Middle East and almost reached India) ignited the minds of medieval explorers, who set their sights of finding the water route to distant India.

Under the orders of the royal courts of Spain and Portugal, organized parties of naval explorers spread beyond the Mediterranean. While Portugal slowly and systematically mapped the western coast of Africa in search of the way to India, Spain took a gamble and accepted to fund the mission of Italian navigator Christopher Columbus, who postulated that India could be reached by sailing to the west. Discovery of the continents of Americas, and Ferdinand Magellan's successful circumvention of the Earth created the biggest wave of human exploration and colonization our world has ever seen. Hundreds of famous explorers scoured across the oceans, in search for undiscovered lands. During that period, entire North and South America were fully mapped, with only few isolated areas remaining uncharted (most notably fabled Northwestern Passage between Canada and Polar Ice, and endless forest around river Amazon). Sadly, this exciting time of exploration also brought destruction of several Native American civilizations, especially in Central America (fall of Aztec and Inca empires).

Explorers from 18th and 19th century focused their work on last remaining two continents – Australia and Africa. During that time, English navigator James Cook travelled several times across the Pacific discovering Australia, Hawaii and searching for the elusive Northwestern Passage, focus of many European explorers was in the central and south Africa. Driven by the increased hostilities before the start of World War I, the entire continent of Africa was conquered and put under European rule. During that time, several explorers found their fame discovering new African lands, most notably David Livingstone.

With every continent of the earth fully mapped, explorers of the 20th century set their sights on only two remaining unmapped parts of the world – North and South Pole. During the time today known as "Heroic Age of Antarctic Exploration", several dozen expeditions went into harsh Pole environments in search for glory and scientific discovery. Most important explorers from that time were Norwegian Roald Amundsen (who first reached the South Pole) and Robert Peary (who first reached North Pole).

The last great area of exploration was created in the second part of 20th century with the development of space travel. Driven by the increased hostilities between United States and Soviet Union, thousands of scientists gave the way for the new breed of explorers to go outside of the confines of the Earth, and visits the world never before seen and touched by humankind. To this day, one of the most important moments in the history of the world is represented by the first space flight by Yuri Gagarin and famous moon landing by Neil Armstrong. Hopefully, advanced science will in the future enable the humankind to further more explore the distant planets of our solar system. ••

# Contents

## Famous English Explorers (9)



## Famous Spanish Explorers (43)

# Famous English Explorers

## 1. William Edward Parry

William Edward Parry (1790-1855), British explorer in the Arctic, who made unsuccessful attempts to find the Northwest Passage and to reach the North Pole. In 1819-20 Parry sailed beyond longitude 11° West, the first person to do so in the Arctic, and discovered and mapped considerable territory, including Barrow Strait, Prince Regent Inlet, Melville Sound, and Wellington Channel. In 1821-23 Parry spent two winters on Melville Peninsula making scientific observations and studying the Inuit. After one more unsuccessful search for the Northwest Passage in 1824-25, he set out in 1827 from Spitsbergen by sledge boat for the North Pole. Before turning back, his party reached latitude 82°45' north, a proximity to the North Pole not attained again until 1876.

## 2. Mark Aurel Stein

Mark Aurel Stein (1862-1943), archaeologist and explorer. Mark Aurel Stein was born in Hungary, and became a British citizen in 1904. He served (1888-99) as principal of the Oriental College, Lahore, India (now in Pakistan), and was superintendent (1910-29) of the Indian Archaeological Survey. Stein also led four major expeditions (1900, 1906-8, 1913-16, 1930) to trace ancient caravan routes between China and the West, concentrating on the little known region of Eastern Turkistan, and did extensive research on the movements of Alexander the Great through Asia. Stein died in Kābul, Afghanistan, while preparing for a new expedition.

## 3. Bartholomew Gosnold

Bartholomew Gosnold (1572-1607), English explorer and colonizer. In 1602 he was in command of the ship Concord, which sailed along the North American coast from Maine to Narragansett Bay. On that voyage he named Cape Cod, some of the islands in Nantucket Sound, including Martha's Vineyard, and the Elizabeth Islands. When he returned to England, Gosnold promoted the establishment of colonies in the areas he had explored and aided the merchants who secured a charter from King James I of England to colonize Virginia. Gosnold was appointed to command the God Speed, one of three ships that transported English settlers in 1606-7 to Jamestown. In 1607 Gosnold was appointed by the king to the council of the colony. After several months in Jamestown he died of fever.

## 4. George Vancouver

George Vancouver (1757-98), British naval officer and explorer, born in King's Lynn, England. He joined the navy at the age of 13 and served with the British explorer Captain James Cook on his second (1772-75) and third (1776-80) voyages. In 1791 Vancouver began an expedition to explore the Pacific coast of North America. He reached his destination in 1792 and spent three years surveying the coast; during this period he became the first European to circumnavigate the island now named Vancouver. In 1795 Vancouver returned to England.

## 5. Sir John Franklin

John Franklin (1786-1847), British rear admiral and explorer of the Arctic and the Northwest Passage.

Franklin was born in Spilsby, Lincolnshire, England. He participated in the battles of Copenhagen in 1801 and Trafalgar in 1805 during the Napoleonic Wars. In 1818 he commanded the Trent in an unsuccessful voyage to the Arctic, and from 1819 to 1822 he commanded an overland expedition commissioned to explore the northern coast of Canada east from the mouth of the Coppermine River. In a subsequent Arctic expedition (1825-27), Franklin traced the North American coastline from the mouth of the Mackenzie River on the Beaufort Sea in northwestern Canada to about the 150th meridian in northeastern Alaska. In 1829 he was knighted and awarded the gold medal of the Geographical Society of Paris. From 1836 to 1843 he was lieutenant governor of Van Diemen's Land (now Tasmania), where he established a college and scientific society. In 1845 he was appointed commander of an expedition to discover the Northwest Passage. The expedition, consisting of the Erebus and the Terror, with 129 officers and men, was last seen by a whaling vessel on July 26, 1845, in Baffin Bay.

Between 1848 and 1859 numerous searching expeditions were dispatched to the Arctic. In July 1857 Lady Jane Franklin, Franklin's second wife, outfitted the Fox, which was finally successful in discovering the history of the ill-fated expedition. The search party obtained from the Inuit in Boothia Peninsula many remains of the Franklin expedition. A record found at Victory Point related details of Franklin's expedition up to April 25, 1848.

According to this record, in 1846 the Erebus and Terror had navigated Peel Sound and Franklin Strait in a southerly direction, but had been stopped by ice between Victoria Island and King William Island. The two ships, icebound from September 1846, had been deserted on April 22, 1848. At that time the total casualties had been 9 officers and 15 men, including Franklin, who had died on June 11, 1847. The surviving members of the party left the ships on April 26, 1848, but apparently perished some days later. Between 1878 and 1880 a U.S. expedition discovered the wreckage of one of Franklin's ships and skeletons of members of his party. A monument commemorating Franklin was erected in 1875 in Westminster Abbey. In the 1980s a Canadian anthropologist, through studies of tissue remains of the crew, determined that they had most likely succumbed to the effects of lead poisoning.

# 6. Mary Henrietta Kingsley

Mary Kingsley (1862-1900), British explorer of West and Central Africa, who was the first European to visit parts of Gabon. Mary Henrietta Kingsley was born in London, the daughter of a medical doctor who travelled extensively. Kingsley made her first visit to Africa in 1893, following the deaths of her parents. She sailed to the Gulf of Guinea port of Calabar, on the coast of what is now Nigeria, and from there travelled inland. From the Niger River region to the north, she travelled southward as far as the lower Congo River region in what is now northern Angola. Throughout the trip she studied African religious practices. She returned to England in 1894.

Kingsley returned to West Africa later that year, stopping first on the coast of what are now Cameroon and Gabon. In Gabon she travelled by steamboat up the Ogooué River. At Lambaréné, she continued her river journey by canoe into the Great Forest region, territory that was then seldom visited by Europeans. After studying the life and culture of the region's Fang people, she returned to the Cameroon coast. Before her return to England in 1895, she climbed Cameroon Mountain (4,095 m/13,435 ft), the area's highest peak.

Kingsley made her final trip to Africa in 1899, planning to visit West Africa again, but the outbreak that year of the Boer War in South Africa led her to travel there instead. While working in Cape Town as a nurse caring for Boer prisoners of war, she contracted typhoid fever and died at the age of 38. Kingsley wrote several books about her experiences in Africa, including *Travels in West Africa* (1897), *West African Studies* (1899), and *The Story of West Africa* (1899).

# 7. Richard Lemon Lander

Richard Lemon Lander (1804-1834), British explorer of West Africa, who determined the true course of the Niger River. Before Lander discovered the river flowed to the Atlantic Ocean, geographers believed that the Niger was a tributary of the Nile River.

Lander was born in Cornwall, England, the son of an innkeeper. When he was 11 years old, he sailed to the West Indies to work for a merchant. In his later teens, Lander saw much of Europe while working as an assistant to travelers. He also visited South Africa. In 1825 the Scottish explorer Hugh Clapperton hired Lander as his assistant on an expedition to determine the course of the Niger. Clapperton died while they were still in the interior of West Africa, leaving Lander as the only surviving European member of the expedition. Lander did not complete the mission, but he managed to reach the coast and returned to England in 1828.

In 1830 the British government commissioned Lander to complete the exploration of the Niger. Accompanied by his brother John, a guide, and a party of porters, Lander headed inland from Lagos, on the coast of present-day Nigeria. They reached the Niger at Bussa and explored upriver for about 160 km (about 100 mi). Heading downstream, they explored the Benue River, the Niger's main tributary, and the Niger's coastal delta. On their way downstream Lander and his brother were taken hostage by the Igbo. Their captors took them down the Niger to the coast, hoping that visiting Europeans there would pay a ransom for their release. But Lander and his brother escaped and found passage away from Africa on a ship bound for Brazil. They returned to England in 1831. Lander's descent of the uncharted section of the Niger from Bussa to its outlet in the Gulf of Guinea revealed that the river did not flow into the Nile, as was once speculated, but to the coast of West Africa and the Atlantic Ocean. In 1832 the Royal Geographical Society awarded Lander a cash prize for this major achievement in African exploration.

Lander returned to West Africa in 1832 to lead trading expeditions up the Niger. Two years later he was wounded in an attack at the inland settlement of Angiama. He managed to return to the coast, but died of his injuries on what is now Bioko Island in Equatorial Guinea. Lander wrote several books, including the story of his expedition up the Niger in Journal of an *Expedition to Explore the Course and Termination of the Niger* (1832).

## 8. Frederick John Dealtry Lugard, 1st Baron Lugard

Frederick Lugard, full name Frederick John Dealtry Lugard, 1st Baron Lugard (1858-1945), British soldier, explorer, and diplomat, who played an important role in Britain's colonial development in Africa. He was instrumental in setting up the British policy of indirect rule, in which colonial governments ruled through indigenous institutions. In 1890 he led an expedition for the British East Africa Company to Uganda, which resulted in British hegemony in the area. Lugard served as governor of Hong Kong from 1907 until 1912, when he returned to Africa. He worked for the unification of Nigeria and was the united colony's first governor (1914-1919). From 1922 to 1936 he was a member of the Permanent Mandates Commission of the League of Nations.

# 9. Harry Hamilton Johnston

Harry H. Johnston, full name Harry Hamilton Johnston (1858-1927), British botanist, explorer, and colonial administrator. He made two botanical expeditions to Africa – to Angola and the Congo River region (1882-83) and to Kilimanjaro (1884) – where he not only collected valuable scientific data but also strengthened British interests in East Africa. After joining the British consular service in 1885, Johnston helped establish the Nyasaland Districts Protectorate in 1891. He served as the British commissioner of the area from 1891 until 1895. In 1893 it was renamed British Central Africa Protectorate, and in 1907 it became Nyasaland Protectorate (present-day Malawi). Johnston also served as a special commissioner in Uganda from 1899 until 1901. He wrote more than 40 books on Africa.

# 10. Sir Richard Burton

Richard Burton was born on March 19, 1821, in the west of England into the family of a ne'er-do-well gentleman soldier and a putative descendant of an illegitimate son of Louis XIV. Soon the family moved to Tours, France, where Burton received a classical education. As a boy, he exhibited courage, derring-do, and a wavering self-control. When he was 10, Burton's family returned briefly to England. He went to school in Richmond, his days punctuated by fighting and wild escapades. Back in France and then in Italy, where Burton spent his adolescent years, his wildness was more characteristic than learning.

Burton attended Trinity College, Oxford, from 1840 to 1842, when he was dismissed for disobedience. Entering the Indian army, he spent the next 7 years studying 11 languages (passing examinations in most and publishing original grammars in 2), practicing his gifts for disguise, learning geodesy, and gathering the material for a book on Goa, two books on Sindh, a discourse on falconry, and a book on bayonet exercise which was ultimately adopted as a British army manual.

In 1852, having begun the courtship of Isabel Arundell which was to result in marriage in 1861, Burton concocted a scheme (he was then on sick leave from the Indian army) to learn the secrets of Mecca and Medina, the jealously guarded shrines of Islam. In April 1853 a bearded Burton stained himself with henna, called himself an Afghani doctor, and for many months sustained the disguise despite varied opportunities of detection. The result of this spectacular exploit was a readable and learned book of travel, *Personal Narrative of a Pilgrimage to Mecca and El Medina* (1855).

## Explorations in Africa

The Arabian adventure whetted Burton's ambitions as an explorer. He turned his attention to the Horn of Africa and, in company with John Speke and others, Burton began an exploration of Somalia and eastern Ethiopia that, for him, culminated in a dangerous foray to the "forbidden" Moslem city-state of Harar, which he was the first white man to visit. Afterward, near Berbera, Burton and Speke had to flee the country after an attack by Somali which left them both wounded. The published account of this African escapade was contained in First Footsteps in East Africa; or An Exploration of Harar (1856).

After participating in the Crimean War, Burton persuaded the Royal Geographical Society in 1855 to appoint him leader of an expedition to ascertain the limits of the "Sea of Ujiji", which had been outlined by missionaries in East Africa, and to "determine the exportable produce of the interior and the enthnography of its tribes." He was urged to seek the source of the Nile and the location of the mountains of the Moon. First Burton visited Kilwa, Mombasa, and the Usambara mountains; these minor exploits formed the basis of Zanzibar: City, Island, and Coast (2 vols., 1872).

Then, in 1857, from Bagamoyo on the Indian Ocean, Burton, Speke, and African guides and porters followed the traditional route to Tabora, where they arrived 10 months later. Burton had begun to suffer intermittent bouts of fever, but he proceeded westward to the trading town of Ujiji, where, early in 1858, he became the first European in modern times to view Lake Tanganyika; what Burton saw was but one of the three components, Lakes Victoria and Nyasa being the others, of the Sea of Ujiji. This was the conclusion of Burton's greatest African performance, appropriately expressed in the lavishly written, intellectually expansive pages of *The Lake Regions of Central Africa* (2 vols., 1860). There are copious notes on the peoples with whom Burton had become acquainted, on the Arab and Indian traders of the interior, on the topography of what was to become Tanganyika, on its flora and fauna, and on a vast miscellany which Burton – a true encyclopedist – had recorded.

After returning to Britain and publishing his book, Burton, by way of diversion, crossed North America, particularly focusing upon the Church of Jesus Christ of the Latter Day Saints (Mormons); The City of the Saints and Across the Rocky Mountains to California (1861) is jammed with random but important information.

## Consular Career and West African Explorations

Burton married Isabel in 1861 and, presumably because of his new responsibilities, decided to take a position in the British consular service. He wanted to go to Damascus but, instead, was offered the comparatively lowly post of consul to the Bights of Benin and Biafra, with a base on Fernando Po. This was known as the Foreign Office grave, but Burton used it to visit Abeokuta, the Egba Yoruba capital in western Nigeria; to climb Mt. Cameroons; to venture up the Gabon River in search of gorillas and to learn about a native people called the Pahouin or Fang; to explore the estuary of the Congo River; and to visit the Portuguese colony of Angola.

In 1864 he paid an official call upon Gelele, King of the Fon of Dahomey. The slave trade still flourished there, and the Foreign Office was determined to negotiate its conclusion. Burton, unhappily, failed to persuade the Fon to cease participating in the trade, but he did acquire a typically full and valuable knowledge of the kingdom, its religion, its culture, and even its Amazons. The published record of these West African years includes a two-volume account of *Nigeria and the Cameroons* (1863), reminiscences of his wanderings throughout the region (1863), *A Mission to Gelele, King of Dahome* (2 vols., 1864), and a book on *Gabon and the Congo* (2 vols., 1876).

Burton spent the rest of his life far from Africa. He was a consul in Brazil, in Damascus, and finally in Trieste. And he wrote, translated, or edited 35 more books, not least of which were his famous translations *The Book of the Thousand Nights and a Night* (10 vols., 1885-1888) and *The Kama Sutra* (1883). He died in Trieste on Oct. 20, 1890.

## 11. Verney Lovett Cameron

Verney Lovett Cameron (1844-1894), British explorer, born near Weymouth and Melcombe Regis, England. Cameron entered the British navy in 1857, and in 1873 he was sent to Africa by the Royal Geographical Society on a second expedition to relieve Scottish missionary and explorer David Livingstone. Soon after the expedition landed at Zanzibar and began its journey inland,

Cameron and his party met servants bearing Livingstone's body. Cameron continued on, becoming the first European to cross tropical Africa from east to west when he reached the Atlantic Ocean in November 1875. On this expedition he found some of Livingstone's papers, which he sent back to England, and also explored the southern half of Lake Tanganyika. When he returned home Cameron was made a commander in the British navy and a companion of the Order of the Bath. In 1878-79 he travelled in Turkey, and in 1882, with British explorer Sir Richard Francis Burton, he visited the African Gold Coast in search of gold. Cameron retired from the navy in 1883 and spent the rest of his life directing commercial projects in Africa. His writings include *Across Africa* (2 volumes, 1877).

## 12. John Hanning Speke

John Speke (1827-1864), British explorer, the first European to sight Lake Victoria and recognize it as the principal source of the Nile River. John Hanning Speke was born near Bideford, in Devon, England, into a wealthy family. At age 17 he joined the British army in India, where he participated in several battles. While abroad, Speke spent time shooting and collecting specimens in the Himalayas and Tibet. In 1854 Speke, who by then considered himself an experienced collector and explorer, headed to Africa to explore. On his way, he met British linguist and explorer Richard Francis Burton in Aden, in southern Arabia (present-day Yemen), and together they planned an expedition to Somalia. Speke arrived in Somalia after Burton, and soon afterward both explorers were wounded in an attack by Somalis. After recovering, Speke fought for Britain in the Crimean War (1853-1856). He then rejoined Burton to explore equatorial Africa in search of the sources of the Nile.

In June 1857 Speke and Burton left the island of Zanzibar for the East African interior. Hardship and illness accompanied them. In February 1858 the expedition sighted Lake Tanganyika, but after discovering that the lake did not empty northward and thus was not a source of the Nile, the party turned back toward Zanzibar. While at rest in Tabora (a village in present-day northwestern Tanzania), the men heard of a massive lake to the north. With Burton ill, Speke made the trip alone and sighted the lake, which he named Victoria Nyanza (Lake Victoria) after the queen of Britain. Based only on its immense size, he declared Lake Victoria to be the source of the Nile.

Burton thought Speke foolish to make such a declaration. However, Speke reached England before Burton, in 1859, and informed the Royal Geographical Society of his "discovery" of the Nile's source. Burton later contested the claim and added other accusations, and a rift developed between the men that would never heal. In 1860 Speke returned to East Africa, accompanied by British army officer James Augustus Grant, and in 1861 he again reached Lake Victoria. This time Speke explored west of the lake and visited the kingdom of Buganda. Unaccompanied by Grant, Speke explored the north end of Lake Victoria. There, in 1862, Speke spotted the falls where the Nile issued from the lake's waters. He named them Ripon Falls after the president of the Royal Geographical Society. Joined again by Grant, Speke proceeded downriver to Khartoum in Sudan and Cairo in Egypt.

Burton and other prominent British explorers and geographers continued to dispute Speke's claim that he had located the Nile's source. In September 1864 the British Association for the Advancement of Science arranged a public meeting for Burton and Speke to debate their views. The day before the event, Speke died while hunting when his gun discharged, apparently accidentally, into his chest. Some speculated, without evidence, that Speke preferred death to facing Burton. Speke's published works include *Journal of the Discovery of the Source of the Nile* (1863) and *What Led to the Discovery of the Source of the Nile* (1864).

# 13. Francis Drake

Francis Drake (1540 - 1596) was one of the most famous naval captains of the 16th century. His numerous exploits brought him great fame and recognition in his home country of England, but also great amount of notoriety by the Spaniards who regarded him as a pirate. As an explorer, he is hailed as a first Englishman that has managed to circumvent the world.

He started his naval career in 1570, with few visits to West Indies as a trader, but two years later he became English privateer and began raiding Spanish ships in the area of the Caribbean. His first naval victory was in 1572 when he successfully raided Spanish town and its harbour, but due to wounds he and his army retreated. A year later he joined with French buccaneer Guillaume Le Testu in an attact that brought them incredible raid. They managed to intercept Spanish mule traders that were carrying 20 tons of silver and gold stolen from the land of Middle America. That kind of bounty could not be easily transported to the 28 kilometres distant shoreline so they decided to burry the majority of the treasure on a secret location. The remainder of a treasure was buried at the shoreline when they noticed that Spaniards were close. A year later Francis Drake returned to England where his fame escalated to new heights.

Following that success in 1577, he received an order from Elizabeth I of England who directed him to go to the South America and explore its lands and defeat any Spain's forces that he encounter. He embarked with a fleet of 6 ships, but only three of them reached the MagellanStrait, but there he was hit with a massive storm that destroyed one of his ships and made one too damaged for the journey ahead. From there he continued north following the cost and raiding Spanish towns reaching the northern parts of Chile. There he managed to capture two Spanish ships that were full of treasure – more than 26tons of silver and several thousands of golden coins and jewels. He travelled to the shores of the North America and then went westward and toward the Asia and Africa.

By 1580, he returned home being the first Englishman who has successfully circumnavigated the Earth. His cargo full of his Spanish treasure secured his success, and in 1581 he received his knighthood, become Mayor of Plymouth and a member in English Parliament.

In the following year Francis Drake performed more military oriented roles, sacking Spanish cities and ports in America (Santo Domingo, Cartagena, fort San Augustin) and destroying Spanish fleets on several occasions (at Cardiz, Corruna, Liberian coast). In 1588, Spanish king launched all-out attack on the England and by then Drake reached the rank of Vice Admiral. He managed to defeat Spanish armada by capturing few key ships and disrupting their formation during the key moments in battle.

After that, he continued his service in English military and died from dysentery at the age of 55 in the year of 1596. He was buried in lead coffin at the sea, and his body is yet to be found.

## 14. Samuel White Baker

Samuel Baker (1821-1893), British traveller and explorer, discoverer of Lake Albert in Africa. Samuel White Baker was born in London and educated in England and Germany. In 1859 and 1860 he superintended the construction of a railway between the Danube River and the Black Sea. In 1861 he and his wife, Florence, set out from Cairo to search for the source of the Nile River. In the Sudan the

Bakers explored Nile tributaries in Ethiopia, determining that the 'Aṭbarah River provided the Nile delta with its fertile soil. In 1862 they proceeded up the Nile to Gondokoro (in the Sudan), where they met British explorers John Hanning Speke and James Augustus Grant. Speke and Grant had left Bagamoyo (now in Tanzania) in 1860, and the former had found Lake Victoria to be the major source of the Nile. Informed by Speke of another lake, said to be crossed by the Nile on its course to Gondokoro, Samuel and Florence Baker continued their journey. Despite hostile slave traders and a mutiny of their troops, on March 14, 1864, they reached the lake and named it Lake Albert, in honour of Prince Albert of Britain.

From 1869 to 1873 Samuel Baker commanded an expedition to suppress slavery and open trade in the equatorial lake region. He explored in Cyprus, Syria, India, Japan, and the United States. He wrote *Eight Years Wandering in Ceylon* (1855), *The Albert Nyanza* (1866), *The Nile Tributaries of Abyssinia* (1867), and *Wild Beasts and Their Ways* (1890).

## 15. Thomas Cavendish

Thomas Cavendish was an English explorer and a privateer that is best remembered as the first man who has deliberately circumvented the Earth. Previous four attempts of circumventions of the globe were not interned as that from their start.

He was born in 1560 at Trimley St. Martin, Suffolk, England as a son of nobleman Roger Cavendish. At 12, he inherited fathers' wealth and around 1585 he purchased ship Elizabeth. He then joined the expedition fleet of Sir Richard Grenville on his journey to Virginia.

Cavendish's first big journey began in 27 June 1586 when he decided to repeat the feat that Francis Drake made in 1577. He built much larger ship called Desire, and together with two ships "Content" and "Hugh Gallant" he started his journey across the world. During their journey, they were prepared to raid any Spanish ships and cities on their way, and that happened when they reached the southern coast of California. They raided 3 Spanish cities and 13 ships including the 600-ton galleon Santa Anna where they captured the biggest treasure that ever fell in English hands.

During his journey across the Pacific Thomas Cavendish learned about the coast of Japan and came in possession of the map of China. With only one ship left, he returned to the England on 9 September 1588 completing his journey for the record time.

Embolden by his newfound glory and wealth he embarked on a second journey across the world on August 1591 with the ships Lester and Desire. They sacked the Brazilian town of Santos and received massive losses at the battle against the Portuguese at the village of Vitória, Espírito Santo. Soon after in 1592 they continued their journey across the Atlantic but according to reports Thomas Cavendish died there near the coast of Ascension Island. John Davis captain of the second ship Desire abandoned the mission and returned to the England.

## 16. James Cook

James was an English explorer, navigator and cartographer that is best known today for his 17th century naval exploits on Pacific Ocean. During his service on English navy, he made three voyages on the pacific where he discovered the Australian continent and islands of Hawaii.

He was born on 7 November 1728 in Marton, Yorkshire, England and in year 1755, he joined the English Navy as a master's mate on HMS Eagle. Three years later, he was a part of a military offensive in the Seven Years' War against the French forces in North America. During that time, he developed considerable skill as a navigator and a cartographer.

His rise trough the ranks continued, and in 1766 Royal Society appointed Cook to go on a mission across the Pacific to record the transit of Venus across the Sun – a very rare astronomical event that happens twice every 243 years. He managed to record that event on 13 April 1769 in Tahiti. After that, he sailed to New Zealand where he managed to map the entire coast of the island. On 19 April 1770, he became first European to spot the eastern shores of the Australia. He successfully returned to England on 12 July 1771 via Cape of Good Hope and the island of Saint Helena.

Cook's second journey started in 1772 when the Royal Society sent him on a mission to search for the mystical island of Terra Australis – landmass that appeared on several ancient European maps. During this trip he was the first explorer that entered the waters of the Arctic Circle, mapped the island South Georgia, visited the Easter Island and almost sailed in the sight of the Antarctica continent. Cook returned to England in 1775 proving that Terra Australis is indeed a myth.

In 1776 James Cook embarked on his last journey with a mission to discover the Northwest Passage – famed sea route that connect the Pacific and Atlantic ocean between the lands of Arctic and northern Canada. Two years later, he becomes the first European to spot the islands of Hawaii, naming them "Sandwich Islands". From there he travelled to the shored of North America and mapped the entire Northern coast up to Alaska and Bering Strait. Frozen Ocean prevented him to sail beyond the Bering Strait which made him decide to abandon the quest for Northwestern Passage. Cook returned to the Hawaii in 1779 where he met with the local people. After making repairs to one of his ship he was involved in a quarrel with the natives that ended with imprisoning the king of Hawaii Kalaniōpuu. That action started the unrest of the locals and eventual death of James Cook by their hands on 14 February 1779.

# 17. Sir Vivian Ernest Fuchs

Vivian Fuchs was an English explorer, who is best known today as a leader of an expedition that first managed to cross Antarctica over land in 1958.

He was born in 1908 in Freshwater, Isle of Wight, England as a son of German Immigrant Ernst Fuchs and Violet Watson. After finishing Cambridge and getting a degree of Geology, he started his life of exploration. He went to Greenland in 1929, visited African lakes in 1930 and Lake Tirukana in 1934. During the Second World War, Fuchs was a part of a Territorial Army on a Gold Coast, and he was a part of a D-Day. After a war, he left the army with the rank of Major and started his scientific work as a geologist with the Falkland Islands Dependencies Survey. There he was involved in early plantings for exploration of Antarctica.

Vivian Fuchs most known journey happened in 1957 when he led the Commonwealth Trans-Antarctic Expedition. Preparations for mission lasted almost three years and they consisted of several advance party scouting and establishment of a Shackleton Base near Vahsel Bay on the Weddell Sea and Scott Base that was supposed to be their destination. On November 24, 1957, he and his party of twelve men started his journey driving specially adapted snow tractors called Sno-Cats. During the travel, they conducted several important scientific measurements – seismic soundings, gravimetric readings and they also measured the thickness of ice that lied over Antarctic continent. Although it was not planed, Fauch decided to change his course and on January 18, he reached the South Pole becoming the third man to reach it over land (after Roald Amundsen in 1911 and Robert Falcon Scott in 1912). After ninety-nine days on ice, they finally reached the Scott Base on 2 March 1958, travelling over 2150 miles.

For his contributions to British scientific discoveries, Vivian Fuchs was knighted by the Queen Elizabeth II. He died on 11 November 1999 in Cambrige at the age of 91.

## 18. Robert Falcon Scott

Robert Falcon Scott was English explorer and Royal Navy officer that is today best remembered for his Polar expeditions during the period of time that is today known as Heroic Age of Antarctic Exploration. Sadly, he died on his second mission shortly after reaching the South Pole. News of his death made him one of the most praised British explorers of his time.

He was born on 6 June 1868 in Stoke Damerel, England as a third child of a brewer and magistrate John Edward. His family had naval tradition, and at age 13 he joined Royal Navy as a cadet training on a ship HMS Britannia. He slowly rose through the ranks, and in 1899 he approached Royal Geographical Society with a wish to lead the Antarctica expedition that was planed in that time. With a newly gained position of Commander, Scott commanded ship Discovery on his first journey to the South Seas, carrying with him famous scientists Ernest Shackleton and Edward Wilson. Scott scouted waters around Antarctica, explored small amount of land and established a small camp that would be used as a starting point for future missions.

When Scott returned to England in 1904, news of his journey fueled his fame and soon after he received promotion to rank of a Captain and many more medals and honours. In 1909, Scott begun planning a new expedition with a goal to reach the South Pole and secure he honour of the British Empire. He embarked on his journey in late 1910, well ahead of his rival Roald Admunsen but several mishaps made him postpone beginning of his land journey. He started his land journey from Ross Island on 1 November

1911, while knowing that that Admunsen's camp was located only 200 miles toward east. His travel proved to be really hard, with severely cold weather that killed all of his travelling ponies. Crew of five finally reached the Pole on 17 January 1912, but there they found out that Admunsen managed to precede them by five weeks. On their journey back, Scott was hit with more bad weather and during those days members of his crew begun slowly to die from cold.

Robert Falcon Scott was last of his crew to die trying to return to his home base on 29 March 1912. His body and tent was found eight months later. News of his death glorified his journey to new heights but in following years news surfaced that he did not plan the mission correctly. Reports spoke that he gave several orders during the journey that worsened his chances of survival.

## 19. Sir Ernest Shackleton

Ernest Shackleton was an Anglo-Irish explorer who is best known for his exploits at Antarctica during the early years of the 20th century. He was one of the key men who explored that region and was responsible for finding the route which was used by first expedition who reached South Pole (Roald Admunsen, 1912).

He was born on 15 February 1874 in Kilkea, County Kildare, Ireland as a son of Henry Shackleton, landowner and a doctor. After finishing Dulwich College, he joined the Royal Navy at the age of 16. Shackleton sailed the seas on various naval merchant ships until the 1901 when he managed to convince several officers to be a member of "Discovery Expedition" fleet that was scheduled to visit Antarctic waters. During those times, they established a land camp and conducted several scientific experiments (first balloon flight over the ice and first use of the sledge dogs on Antarctic). Sadly, in 1903, his health becomes weakened by the cold weather and he was sent home by HMS Morning.

Four years later in 1907 Shackleton was chosen to be a leader in a new Antarctic expedition with a mission to explore deeper into continent. He reached the land on 29 January 1908 and after many delays, Shackleton started his land journey to south on 19 October. After three months on the road, they managed to come only 112 miles from the pole, but diminishing rations made them decide to turn back. In England Shackleton become true public hero, and on 12 July 1909, King Edward VII made him to be Commander of the Royal Victorian Order and a knight. In the following few years he shared his experiences from the Antarctica, and several of his peers (Robert Falcon Scott and Roald Amundsen) used them in their journeys to the Pole in 1912.

After hearing that Pole was reached Shackleton begun preparing a mission in which he planed to cross the entire continent of Antarctica from one side to the other while visiting the Pole. Original plan was that Shackleton will start journey with ship "Endurance" and another ship "Aurora" would wait for them on the other side of Antarctic, but troubles soon changed those plans. On 19 January 1915, "Endurance" became frozen in ice and Shackleton soon realized that they would not be able to get free from it until spring. They remained stuck there until 21 November when ship finally sunk under the ice. Survivors made a camp on ice, hoping that water current will bring them closer to the 400km distant Paulet Island. On 9 April, their ice started braking and Shackleton ordered his crew to try to reach land in small rescue boats. After five rough days on the sea and 497 days after they left Europe, they managed to travel over 90km to the shore of the small inhospitable Elephant Island. From there Shackleton formed a five-man crew with task to reach the South Georgia whaling stations and search for help. After almost three weeks on the sea, he finally reached whaling station at Stromness. From there he formed the rescue party which successfully evacuated all of his crew stranded on Elephant Island.

After he returned home, Shackleton joined the British Army during the World War one. In 1920 he embarked on another mission that was supposed to chart the islands surrounding the arctic continent, but on January 1922, Shackleton suffered fatal heart attack near the coast of the island South Georgia.

## 20. Ranulph Fiennes (Ran Fiennes)

Ranulph Fiennes is a British adventurer and novelist who is best known today for his various exploits around the world. He is especially hailed for being the first man to cross the Antarctica from one side to the other [via the pole] on foot. He holds several Guinness World Records and as an author, he released over a dozen fiction and non-fiction books, most notably biography of famous explorer Captain Robert Falcon Scott.

Fiennes was born on 7 March 1944 in Glasgow, Scotland, but he spent his youth in South Africa. After serving the Royal Army with Royal Scots Greys and Special Air Service, Fiennes began his life as an adventurer. He sailed across the White Nile in a hovercrafts (1969), explored Norway's Jostedalsbreen Glacier. His most ambitious adventure started in 1979, when he and his two friends Oliver Shepard and Charles Burton started the "Transglobe Expedition". They went from Greenwich England to the desert of Sahara, jungles of Mali and the Ivory Coast, and reached South Africa at Cape Town. From there they sailed to Antarctica and crossed it from one side to another visiting South Magnetic Pole. Next, they visited Australia, western shores of America, northern Canada and from there they successfully walked over Arctic visiting North Pole. On August 29 1982, they successfully returned to Greenwich completing their 100.000-mile long route across the globe.

In following years, Fiennes led an expedition that discovered the lost city of Ubar in Oman. Fiennes also tried two times to cross Antarctica and one time Arctic on foot without any aid. He failed on all three attempts and managed to be evacuated to safety. On May 2009, Fiennes successfully climbed on the summit of Mount Everest becoming the oldest British person to achieve that goal.

In 1993, Ranulph Fiennes was awarded with Order of the British Empire for his endeavors and contributions with charities.

## 21. Sir Humphrey Gilbert

Sir Humphrey Gilbert (1537-1583) was an English adventurer, explorer, politician, and soldier that lived during the 16th century Tudor era. During his life he became well-known noble of English crown, and as a half-brother to the famous Sir Walter Raleigh he also forged his reputation as a pioneer of English colonization in North America.

Humphrey Gilbert was born in Devon, as a fifteenth son of Otho and Katherine Champernowne Gilbert. After he finished his naval and military education at the University of Oxford, he joined the fight against Irish rebellion led by Shane O'Neill, but he soon found himself in London, where he remained close to the English crown. After the end of the rebellion, he was appointed to the office of Ulster and as a member of the Irish parliament. During his stay there, he fought many battles against rebellious Irish.

In early 1570s, Gilbert returned to England where he married Anne Aucher and set his sights on the colonization of Greenland. Several of his expeditions sadly never had any result – in 1577 Forbisher's trip failed to explore Greenland, in 1578 Gilbert himself unsuccessfully went to Americas, and in 1579 he led failed sea campaign against Ireland. However, with the end of his six year license to explore the waters and lands of Newfoundland slowly coming to expire, he managed to gather the funds and form the fleet of five exploratory ships. Sadly, dreams of the crew and the funders of the trip were shattered with the Gilbert's poor planning. He did not pay taxes on the newfound lands before embarking on a trip, thus making all their discoveries and claimed land illegal, and his rag-tag crew of misfits, criminals and ex-pirates gave much problems before the fleet somehow managed to reach Newfoundland.

Humphrey Gilbert and his fleet did not manage to secure permanent settlement on the Newfoundland. Burdened by the harsh lands and lack of supplies, entire fleet left for the England, but during the way back nearly all of his ships were damaged during strong storms and poor navigation.

On September 9th of 1583, his flagship frigate "Squirrel" succumbed to the sea during the one storm, taking to the deeps the lives of Sir Humphrey Gilbert and every member of his crew.

## 22. Sir John Hawkins

Sir John Hawkins (1532 - 1595) was a famous English shipbuilder, military commander, merchant and a slave trader that left his mark on naval history during the second part of 16th century. During his life he proved himself to be very accomplished military tactician by organizing defense of England against overwhelming forces of Spanish Armada in 1588, and by starting an era of organized English slave transport from the shores of Africa to America. Hawkins spent majority of his career working with other famous explorers of his time – Sir Francis Drake, Sir Walter Raleigh, Sir Richard Grenville and his son Sir Richard Hawkins.

John Hawkins was born in England as fourth son of William Hawkins and Joan Trelawney, and second cousin of Sir Francis Drake. As his family consisted from the line of extremely wealthy merchants, John continued that tradition and begun his merchant career. In 1555 he formed syndicate of merchants with a goal to transport slaves from Africa to new World. On his first journey, he travelled with three ships and one captured Portuguese ship, successfully delivering 301 slaves on the shores of Caribbean and managing to anger the Spanish who promptly forbid the travel of English slave ships in West Indies waters.

Second journey John Hawkins was even more ambitious, and using his newly added 700-ton ship "Jesus of Lubeck" he ransacked the coast of Africa, capturing over 400 slaves and destroying several Portuguese and Spanish settlements along the way. After successfully selling his slaves in the Columbian city Rio de la Hacha (against the wishes of protesting Spanish), he gathered his profit and returned to England in 1566. Third journey performed between 1567 and 1569 was initially even more prosperous, but upon entering the Central American waters, Hawkins became entangled in the conflict between Spanish crown and Spanish colonist. In the ensuing battles, only two of his ships survived, and Hawkins managed to return to England with only two ships.

After those 3 journeys, John Hawkins focused more on his political and shipbuilding career. He helped Queen Elizabeth in 1571 in finding traitors that helped Ridolfi plot, which brought him many honours and eventually position of Treasurer of the Royal Navy in 1578. His management of fleet proved to be very instrumental in organization of the navy, and his shipbuilding made even smaller ships very effective in combat. All those changes introduced by him paid off in 1588 when overwhelming force of Spanish Armada set sail for English waters. During that time, John Hawkins was one of the three main commanders that organized defense of England, together with his Francis Drake and Martin Frobisher. Immediately following that battle, Sir John Hawkins (now knighted by the English crown) and Francis Drake formed exploratory fleet with a goal to find Spanish treasure fleets and prevent King Philip II's efforts to re-arm his fleet. Sadly, English expedition utterly failed, and enabled Spanish to regain much of the lost power in the next decade.

The last expedition of Sir John Hawkins happened in 1595. Joined forces of Sir John Hawkins and Sir Francis Drake travelled across West Indies, attacking any Spanish forces and looking for gold and riches. On their journey they launched two unsuccessful attacks on San Juan in Puerto Rico, until late 1595 when both of the captains fell ill from dysentery and died on the sea. Bodies of both of them were buried on the sea off the coast of Puerto Rico and Porto Belo, while Hawkins' son Sir Richard Hawkins assumed command over the remaining fleet.

Sir John Hawkins is today remembered for his exploits, especially after 2006's publishing of the book that covered his life and influence on the slave trade. His journeys are also remembered for the first introduction of potatoes and tobacco to England, and the birth of the word "shark" (which was brought to the Europe by Hawkins sailors).

## 23. Sir Martin Frobisher

Sir Martin Frobisher was a famous English seamen, privateer and explorer that is today best remembered for unsuccessful exploration of Northwestern Passage and gold mining career.

Frobisher was born between 1535 or 1539 in Altofts, Yorkshire, and between 1560 and 1561 he formed his initial plans to find the elusive Northwestern Passage – trade route between North America and Artic that could potentially greatly benefit trade between Europe, North America and India. After 5 years of gathering resources, he finally procured necessary funding's and crew for this three borrowed ships. He set sail on June 1576, and quickly lost one of his ship in a sudden and violent storm. Even though his journey was unsuccessful, he brought home with him a peace of black ore for which he suspected it contained gold.

Second voyage of Martin Frobisher received much more attention, financial backing and government support. Larger fleet was assembled, and Frobisher received permission to claim any newfound land as his own. Even though discovery of Northwestern passage was one of the objectives of this voyage, majority of its time was used by full complement of miners and equipment that collected around 200 tons of soil. After slow journey home, English crown welcomed Frobisher and started evaluating the newfound land for gold.

Even though the amount of found gold was low, English crown still held hope that newfound lands in Canada still have major gold mining potential. Because of that, Frobisher received commission for his third and final expedition, this time equipped with 15 ships. During the expedition, many problems prevented the settlers to build permanent settlement, and after return to England majority of the scil was deemed worthless. Some of the cost of the mission was eventually recouped by selling the found Iron Pyrite.

With another unsuccessful journey behind him, Frobisher fell out from the Crown's grace. He spent several following years as a privateer and pirate, fighting against the Spanish. Together with Sir Francis Drake he managed to win several notable battles against the Spanish. Hostilities between England and Spain finally reached highpoint in the summer of 1588 when armada of 132 Spanish ships set sail toward the England, and clashed against 34 English warships and 163 armed merchant vessels. After winning the battle, English crown knighted several captains of their ships, including Martin Frobisher.

In the years after the end of the battle against Spanish Armada, Frobisher continued his privateer activities on the sea. On November 22, 1594, Sir Martin Frobisher died during one of his raids on Spanish Fortresses on the coast of Brittany.

# 24. Sir Richard Grenville

Sir Richard Grenville (1542 - 1591) was an English sea captain and explorer that is today best remembered for his involvement in colonizing New World and several famous fights against Spanish forces. As a cousin of famous explorers and Privateers Sir Walter Raleigh and Sir Francis Drake, Richard Grenville managed to forge his own fame by taking his stand in the Battle of Flores, where he fought and died against overwhelming odds. To this day, he is immortalized in poem "*The Revenge*", written by the Tennyson.

Little is known about the early life of Richard Grenville, except that he was born 5 June 1542 at Buckland Abbey in Devon, England. 22 years later he married Mary St. Leger, fought a short campaign against the Turks in Hungary and entered the political life by taking several posts within English and Irish governments. By 1577 Richard Grenville received his knighthood and position of sheriff of Cornwall, but he wanted excitement on the sea and joined the fleet of his cousin Sir Walter Raleigh and begun helping him in his exploration of North America. In 1584 he commanded the fleet of several Raleigh's ships, and one year later he took four ships to the shores of Virginia where they made permanent settler colony. On his return to England he even managed to capture one Spanish ship and ransack Azores, for which he received position of Vice-Admiral of the navy.

By 1588 war between Spanish and England reached highpoint when armada of 132 Spanish ships started their attack on the badly defended English fleet. During that summer Sir Walter Raleigh & Sir Richard Grenville were both responsible for the coordination of the land based defense in Devon and Cornwall, but the eventual destruction of Spanish Armada at the sea prevented their troops from seeing any action.

The last war campaign of Richard Grenville came in 1591, when he and Lord Thomas Howard were sent by English crown to sail to Azores in search of Spanish treasure fleet. During their journey they encountered vast Spanish war armada which quickly surrounded them and forced them to fight. Sir Richard commanded his flagship galleon "Revenge" (often considered to be one of the best made warships of its time) with incredible tactics, fighting alone against incredible force of 53 Spanish ships and causing serious damage to the 15 enemy galleons. The power of his command over his crew was so great that they continued to fight until very end of their resources, until last barrel of powder and last working piece of weapon. After 12 hours of battle Sir Richard Grenville was adamant to destroy his ship in defiance, his crew surrendered against his wishes and everyone became prisoner of war.

Several days later, on 10th September 1591, Sir Richard Grenville died from the wounds that he sustained in the battle, cursing the cowardice of his crew until his last breath. Spaniards heavy losses sustained during the battle against Sir Richard were heavily multiplied soon after, when very strong week long storm destroyed 15 of their ships, including the captured "Revenge".

## 25. Sir Richard Hawkins

Sir Richard Hawkins (1562 - 1622) was an English admiral, privateer and explorer who is today best remembered as a son of a Admiral Sir John Hawkins and a nephew of famous Sir Francis Drake. During his life he accompanied them into their discoveries around the world, and took part in the defense of England against Spanish Armada in 1588.

Richard Hawkins was born in Plymouth, England as a son of Elizabethan explorer Sir John Hawkins, and accompanied his father from early age sailing between Europe and New Indies regularly. During that time he educated himself in the art of naval warfare, trade and exploration, learning from his father, Sir Francis Drake and Sir Walter Raleigh. Before taking command of warship that defended the waters of England against Spanish Armada in 1588, Hawkins took part in several travels to New Indies, most notably visit to Brazil in 1585 and Sir Walter Raleigh's colony Ralph Lane in 1586.

After the end of hostilities against the Spanish, Richard Hawkins and his father formed another expedition to West Indies, this time setting their sights on the Spanish Main that lay beyond Strait of Magellan. During his stay there he engaged Spanish several times until his eventual wounding and capturing in 1594 in Chile. He remained in their imprisonment for several years, until English government ransomed him for £3000. Upon returning to England in 1603 he was knighted by King James I, and become Lord Mayor of Plymouth and spent next 17 years on land.

In 1620 he again stepped to the command of the ship, and led the military fleet against the Mediterranean pirates that operated from North African coast of Algeria (Barbary).

Sir Richard Hawkins died in London on 17 April 1622, and he remained remembered for his widely successful and popularized book "*Voyage into the South Sea*".

## 26. Sir Walter Raleigh

Sir Walter Raleigh (1554-1618) was English aristocrat and explorer that is today best remembered for his journey to the South America where he searched for the legendary lost city of gold – El Dorado. His exploits greatly popularized both the myths of this ancient city and the European usage of the South American plant called tobacco.

During his life he made three famous journeys across Atlantic – once as a leader of the private owned fleet of ships that colonized the lands of North America (today located across Virginia and North Carolina), and two times as a leader of the expedition fleet in South America.

Walter Raleigh was born in Devon, England, as a son of Walter Raleigh and Catherine Champernowne. He first became known already as a grown man after the successful suppression of rebellion in the Ireland and the Siege of Smerwick. By that time he became land owner who quickly rose through the ranks of English nobility with the help of the Queen Elizabeth I. With the help of the royal patent, Raleigh successfully led the privately owned colonization fleet to the shores of the North America where they settled on the lands of Virginia. For that successful mission English crown knighted him in 1985, and gave him several notable holdings and positions (such as warden of the mines of Cornwall and Devon, Lord Lieutenant of Cornwall, Vice-Admiral, and a member of the British parliament in 1585 and 1586). Almost all of that came to end in 1591 after he married one of her personal ladies in waiting without permission, thus breaking the Queen's law.

In 1594, three years after his imprisonment in the Tower of London for defying the Crown with his wedding, he came to the information that South American river of Caroní is hiding the remains of the ancient city that was made from gold. Emboldened by his research, he quickly formed the exploratory fleet and in the same year sailed across the Atlantic. Although Raleigh never found not a single concrete shred of evidence of the city's existence, his return to England was quickly followed with the publication of the book "*The Discovery of Guiana*" in which he greatly exaggerated the events that happened during his journey. Even after many of the claims in the book were proven to be false, "*The Discovery of Guiana*" played a very important role in the popularization of the myth of the El Dorado.

After this unsuccessful journey, Sir Walter Raleigh continued to serve English crown. He was a part in the 1956s capture of Spanish city Cádiz, and the movement of the English fleets against the Portuguese forces in the Azores in 1957. Events of those few years repaired his relations to the English crown, and he quickly returned to the political life. After serving as a parliament for Dorset, Governor of the Channel Island of Jersey, Raleigh was again arrested after the accusations of his involvement in the Main Plot against King James in 1603. He masterfully defended himself during the trial, and managed to win his freedom in 1616, the same year he departed for the South America for the second time. His second journey again proved to be unsuccessful, and during the expedition his forces managed to ransack Spanish outpost town of San Tomé on the Orinoco River. This attack proved to be fatal for Sir Walter Raleigh. His son died during the battle with the Spanish, and Raleigh himself received similar fate after his return to England after Spanish ambassador Count Gondomar successfully demanded for his death sentence.

Sir Walter Raleigh was executed by decapitation in the Old Palace Yard at the Palace of Westminster on 29 October 1618. Many of the present nobility and citizens had good relation to Raleigh, and regarded his death as unnecessary and unjust.

# Famous Spanish Explorers

# 1. Francisco Vasquez de Coronado

Francisco Vasquez de Coronado (1510 - 1554) was a Spanish conquistador and explorer who is today remembered for his visits to New Mexico and parts of southwestern United States in mid-16th century. During the majority of his life he strived to find the mystical Seven Cities of Gold, which are today better known by the name El Dorado.

Coronado was born in Salamanca, Spain, as a son of wealthy Juan Vásquez de Coronado y Sosa de Ulloa and Isabel de Luján Juan Vásquez. After spending 25 years with his family, Coronado finally set to seas with the son of his father's patron, Antonio de Mendoza. After they reached Mexico, Coronado married Beatriz de Estrada, with whom he had eight children. During his early life he managed to conquer the area of Kingdom of Nueva Galicia (todays northwest of Mexico). It was during that time that he sent Friar Marcos de Niza into expedition north (into today's New Mexico), who came back to Coronado bringing the stories of a wealthy city, created from gold, sitting on a hill that overlooked pacific ocean.

Emboldened by this story, Francisco Vasquez de Coronado formed a large expedition that had a goal to explore lands of northwestern Mexico. Separated in two groups (one travelling by land, and one carrying supplies over the rivers), Coronado led the force of over 300 Spaniards and 1300 natives in search of El Dorado. During 1540 and 1541 Coronado travelled over much unexplored lands, following several leads, all leading into failure. After his patience came to an end in late 1541, one of the Indian guides that claimed the cities were real finally confessed that his stories were false. This realization finally gave reason to stop the search, and after spending winter on the banks of the river Rio Grande, expedition finally started its way home on April 1542.

Unsuccessful end of his exploratory mission brought many troubles to Francisco Vasquez de Coronado. In the following years he fell from the grace of local rulers, lived through public humiliation after his atrocities toward Indian slaves came to light, and received several demotions that finally left him working in a minor position in Mexico City.

Francisco Vasquez de Coronado died on 22 September 1554, at the age of 44.

## 2. Hernando de Soto

Hernando de Soto (1496 - 1542) was a Spanish conquistador and explorer that is today best remembered for his exploration of Florida and landmass of southeastern United States. During his exploration of North America (then believed to be Eastern Asia), he encountered the river Mississippi, becoming the first European who crossed it.

De Soto was born in either Barcarrota or Badajoz, in Extremadura, Spain as a son of the middle class family of hidalgos (Spanish nobility). After his initial education that lasted to his age of 14, he joined the military. Several years later Spanish finished their long lasting conflict against the Moors and the Islamic lands in Iberian Peninsula, and majority of Spanish youth and military personel set their sights on exploring, claiming the newfound lands and finding glory in New Indies, which were discovered several decades ago.

In 1514, at the age of 18, De Soto boarded the ship and sailed to the west with first Governor of Panama, Pedrarias Dávila. During the several next years he took part in several important exploratory missions in both North and South America. Between his arrival and 1530 he explored the South America (Panama) where he received his first command over ship, charted the waters around Nicaragua with Francisco de Cordoba, and was engaged in profitable slave trade between Africa and Nicaragua.

In 1530, Hernando de Soto was recruited by famous explorer and conquistador Francisco Pizarro in his mission to Peru. During that journey, Pizarro and De Soto invaded the Incan empire, captured emperor of the Incas Atahuallpa and killed several thousand of his people in search for gold. Their atrocities in the end paid off when Emperor Atahuallpa offered his ransom – enough gold to fill the space of his 22 foot prison room, from bottom to as high he could reach. Sadly after collecting their gold, they strangled the last Incan ruler and went to establish the city of Lima, which was later on used as a staging point in destruction of Incan capitol Cusco.

After the conquest of Incas, Hernando De Soto returned to Spain carrying his share of gold and brining news of his and Francisco Pizarro's successful mission. As a result of his newfound riches and honours, he settled in Seville, married Ines de Bobadilla, and started preparing the plans for his next mission to the West Indies. After gathering the force of 10 ships, and 950 soldiers, he left Spain on April 6, 1538 and after serving a year in Cuba as a governor he finally reached the lands of Florida in May of 1539. He explored the lands of Florida and South East America for four years, searching the gold and violently exterminating any opposition from the local natives.

He breathed his last on May 21, 1542 after being sick from fever. He was buried at the bank of the river Mississippi.

## 3. Juan Ponce de Leon

Juan Ponce de Leon (1474 - 1521) was a Spanish explorer who is today best remembered for his discoveries in the North America. He was one of the first European who entered Gulf of Mexico and a leader of a first expedition that set foot on Florida. In addition to his exploration, he gathered considerable fame as a successful politician, noble, governor and was very influential in spreading the myth of the Fountain of Youth, for which he claimed was located in Florida.

Juan Ponce de Leon was born in Santervas, Spain sometimes between 1460 and 1474 as a son of a wealthy and noble family.

After finishing his education by learning several languages, physics, geometry, mathematics and astronomy he joined the court of Spanish royal family where he served as a page to Pedro Nunuz de Guzman, Knight Commander of military order of Calatrava. During early 1490s he travelled the seas as a privateer, fighting against Moors in the Atlantic. However, after the hostilities ended, he found himself bored with the life on the land. Seeing incredible potential in the recent discovery made by Christopher Columbus, he grabbed the first chance he got and joined Columbus on his second journey to West Indies in 1493. After several years at the sea, Juan Ponce de Leon gained significant knowledge about naval life. He visited Hispaniola where he confronted hostile native Indians, searched for gold in Haiti, and even founded a Spanish settlement there. When Columbus decided that it is time for his return back to Europe in late 1494, Juan Ponce de Leon decided to stay and try to use his newfound knowledge to expand his wealth.

His patience finally paid off 18 years later when he received permission from Spanish king Charles V to explore modern day Bahamas and seize the newfound lands as his own. During that time Ponce founded the city of Puerto Rico, and explored the sea near Florida. After returning to Puerto Rico he successfully won another grant which empowered him to seize the lands in the newfound Florida. Equipped with the crew of two ships, he successfully colonized Florida by establishing first city on its grounds. During the building of that settlement, crew of Ponce de Leon expedition became under attack from hostile native Indians. Wounded from the poisoned arrow, Ponce quickly travelled to Havana, where he eventually died from his battle wounds.

Juan Ponce de Leon is today remembered for his discoveries in the Central America, establishment of the famous city of Puerto Rico and his lifelong desire to find the Fountain of Youth.

# 4. Juan de la Cosa

Juan de la Cosa was a Spanish explorer and cartographer best-known for his 15th century voyages with Christopher Columbus in which they discovered the lands of Americas. He was born in 1460. in Sta. Maria del Puerto, Canrabria Spain and from his early live he lived by the water. Before his voyages to the New World he made several travels in Mediterranean and one expedition to the West Coast of Africa.

In 1492 Juan de la Cosa joined Christopher Columbus on his voyage to the America as the owner and master of the expedition flagship "Santa Maria". Almost five months later his ship sunk near the coast of Haiti, an event for which Christopher Columbus blamed him. On a next two voyages De la Cosa commanded ships "Marigalante" and "La Niña". At that time he started making maps of the new land they encountered.

In 1499 he embarked on his fourth journey with Alonso de Ojeda and Amerigo Vespucci. They explored the coast of South American continent from Essequibo River to Cape Vela. During this expedition he made the first map of the known lands of the "New World", a map called "Mappa Mundi" that will make him considerably famous in Europe. It represented the first undisputed map of the lands of Americas.

His fifth voyage happened one year later in 1500, when he, Rodrigo de Bastidas and Vasco Núñez de Balboa explored the lands of Colombia, Panama and the western coast of South America. Upon his return on Haiti in 1502, he was tasked with the job of delegate in the Spanish dispute against Portugal regarding the rights of the some newly discovered land. During the negotiations he was incarcerated by the Portugal, but soon after he was liberated by the help of Spanish Queen Isabella.

On his next voyage he embarked on his own, carrying settlers to the Pearl Islands and Gulf of Uraba, but he also visited lands of Jamaica and Haiti.

His last seventh voyage started in 1509 when De la Cosa carried two hundred settlers on three ships to the coast of Haiti. There he joined his fleet with Alonso de Ojeda and Francisco Pizarro, and after few disputes they landed their ships in the area where is currently located Columbian city Cartagena. Soon after hostile Indians attacked their camp and killed De la Cosa with several poison arrows. Alonso de Ojeda managed to flee to his anchored fleet in Turbaco where he carried the news of Juan de la Cosa's death.

## 5. Sebastian de Ocampo

Sebastián de Ocampo was a Spanish explorer and navigator that is best-known for this discoveries during the 16th century called as the Age of Discovery.

Under the order of the governor of Hispaniola, in 1508 Ocampo embarked on the journey that will make him famous. Before his journey everyone assumed that the land that laid west of the island of Hispaniola called Cuba was a part of Indian continent, and several maps portrayed this land with much larger landmass (even the maps created by Christopher Columbus, and others after him). Ocampo proved them wrong when he managed to circumnavigate it and thus he confirmed that Cuba is indeed an island. He is also the first European who have entered the waters of Gulf of Mexico.

Exact date of his birth and death is not known although it is suspected that he died of old age.

# 6. Vasco Nunez de Balboa

Vasco Núñez de Balboa was a Spanish explorer and conquistador that is best-known for his exploits and discoveries in the early years of the 16th century. Today he is remembered as the fist European that reached the Pacific Ocean.

He was born in 1475 in Jerez de los Caballeros in Badajoz, Spain as the third or fourth son of the nobleman father Nuño Arias and mother Lady de Badajoz. Encouraged by the news of the Christopher Columbus discovery he embarked on a journey to the New World in 1500, and after five years of exploring Mexican gulf he settled in Hispaniola. There he lost of his wealth by being a farmer, but soon he returned to the sea, and eventually joined the crew of the captain Fernández de Enciso. Together they searched for a place to form a new settlement and after few confrontations with hostile natives, they managed to secure a land on the west side of the Gulf of Mexico. There in 1510 Badajoz founded the first European settlement on the American soil, a city called Santa María la Antigua del Darién.

In the following few years, he continued to plunder the lands of Middle America and in 1513 he heard the first rumours of the "other sea" with rich golden deposits that lay across the land of west Panama. Even when he received news that Spain will not help him in this discovery, he assembled the crew and started his journey on September 1 1513. He travelled by canoes across the Isthmus of Panama, a small strip of land that lies between Caribbean and Pacific, and on September 25th he reached the Pacific. He named it "Mar del Sur" (SouthSea) but seven years later Magellan renamed it to Pacific Ocean because of its calm waters.

Vasco Núñez de Balboa died by decapitation in 1519 while being imprisoned on the Santa Maria, death that was brought to him by the dispute with several governors of that area (notably Francisco Pizarro and Pedro Arias de Ávila).

## 7. Hernando de Alarcön

Hernando de Alarcón (flourished 16th century), Spanish navigator and explorer in America. On May 9, 1540, Alarcón sailed to the head of the Gulf of California and completed the explorations begun by the Spanish explorer Francisco de Ulloain the preceding year. During this voyage Alarcón proved to his satisfaction that no open-water passage existed between the Gulf of California and the South Sea, or Pacific Ocean. Subsequently he entered the Colorado River, which he named the Buena Guia. He was the first European to ascend the river for a distance considerable enough to make important observations. On a second voyage he probably proceeded past the present site of Yuma, Arizona. A map drawn by one of Alarcón's pilots is the earliest accurately detailed representation of the gulf and the lower course of the river.

## 8. Diego de Almagro

Diego de Almagro (1475-1538), Spanish soldier and adventurer, born in Almagro, near Ciudad Real. He went to the New World in 1514, and settled in Panama City five years later. In 1524 he formed a partnership with the Spanish explorer Francisco Pizarro to explore and conquer the region on the coast of the Pacific Ocean south of Panama, which was reported to hold deposits of gold. In their first two expeditions (1524-1525 and 1526-1528), although beset by great hardships, they learned of the wealth of the Inca Empire. In 1529 Pizarro was granted authority by the Holy Roman emperor Charles V to conquer and rule Peru, and in 1533 the partners completed the conquest of the country. In 1535 Charles V appointed Almagro governor of New Toledo, an area lying south of Pizarro's grant and including the northern portion of present-day Chile. After invading and subjugating his lands in 1535-1536, Almagro claimed that Cuzco, the ancient Inca capital, lay within his region and entered the city as the legitimate governor. Consequently, a civil war broke out between the followers of Almagro and those of Pizarro. Attempts to negotiate a peaceful settlement were unsuccessful, and in 1538 Almagro was defeated and executed on Pizarro's orders.

## 9. Pedro de Alvarado

Pedro de Alvarado (1486-1541), Spanish explorer, born in Badajoz. In 1518 he accompanied the Spanish explorer Juan de Grijalva on his voyage along the coast of Mexico. In 1519 he was second in command to the Spanish adventurer Hernán Cortés on their voyage from Havana and took an active part in the conquest of Mexico. He conquered and settled Guatemala in 1523-24 and in 1534 headed an expedition to claim the territory of Quito, maintaining it had not been included in the grant made to the Spanish conqueror of Peru, Francisco Pizarro. Met by Pizarro's troops, he agreed to turn back upon the payment of a large indemnity. Alvarado was killed during a Native American rebellion in Mexico.

# 10. Álvar Nüôez Cabeza de Vaca

Álvar Núñez Cabeza de Vaca (1490-1557), Spanish explorer, born ın Jerez de la Frontera. In 1527 he was appointed treasurer of a royal expedition of about 300 men led by the Spanish soldier Pánfilo de Narváez to conquer and colonize Florida. The expedition sailed into Tampa Bay about April 1528, began an overland march to Apalachee Bay, and then attempted to reach Mexico. During the next two years more than half the men died, and Cabeza de Vaca emerged as the leader. He led a small band of survivors to an island, possibly Galveston Island, off the southwestern coast of what is now Texas, where the band was captured by Native Americans. Early in 1535, Cabeza de Vaca and the three other survivors of the expedition escaped and began a trek through what are now the southwestern United States and northern Mexico. In 1536 the four men reached a Spanish settlement on the Sinaloa River in Mexico. Cabeza de Vaca returned to Spain in 1537 and was rewarded with an appointment as governor of Río de la Plata (now largely Paraguay).

In 1541-42 Cabeza de Vaca led an expedition 1609 km (1000 mi) through the south of present-day Brazil to Asunción, the capital of Río de la Plata. He took office as governor of the province in 1542 but was ousted two years later as the result of a revolt. Recalled to Spain under arrest in 1554, he was later banished to Africa. In 1556 he obtained a pardon and a pension. His account of the Narváez expedition, Relación (1542), and his tales of the Zuni and their villages, the legendary Seven Cities of Cíbola, encouraged other expeditions to America, notably those of the explorers Hernando de Soto and Francisco Vásquez de Coronado.

# 11. Hernän Cortës

Hernán Cortés or Hernando Cortez (1485-1547), Spanish explorer and conqueror of the Aztec Empire of Mexico. Cortés was born in Medellín, Extremadura. He studied law at the University of Salamanca but cut short his university career in 1501 and decided to try his fortune in the Americas. Cortés sailed for Santo Domingo (now the Dominican Republic) in the spring of 1504. In 1511 he joined Spanish soldier and administrator Diego Velázquez in the conquest of Cuba and subsequently became alcalde (mayor) of Santiago de Cuba. In 1518 Cortés persuaded Velázquez, who had become governor of Cuba, to give him the command of an expedition to Mexico. The mainland had been discovered the year before by Spanish soldier and explorer Francisco Fernández de Córdoba and subsequently by Juan de Grijalva, nephew of Velázquez.

On February 19, 1519, Cortés, with a force of some 600 men, fewer than 20 horses, and 10 field pieces, set sail from Cuba. He left despite the cancellation of his commission by Velázquez, who had become suspicious that Cortés, once in a position to establish himself independently, would refuse to recognize his authority. Cortés sailed along the coast of Yucatán and in March 1519 landed in Mexico, subjugating the town of Tabasco. From the native inhabitants of Tabasco, Cortés learned of the Aztec Empire and its ruler, Montezuma II.

Cortés took numerous captives, one of whom, Malinche (baptized Marina), became his mistress; out of loyalty to him she acted as the interpreter, guide, and counselor for the Spaniards. Finding a better harbour a little north of San Juan, the Spaniards moved there and established a town, La Villa Rica de la Vera Cruz (now Veracruz). Cortés organized an independent government, and renouncing the authority of Velázquez, acknowledged only the supreme authority of the Spanish crown. In order to prevent those of his small force who opposed this movement from deserting him and carrying the news to Cuba, Cortés destroyed his fleet.

After negotiations with Montezuma, who tried to persuade Cortés not to enter the Aztec capital city of Tenochtitlán, Cortés started his famous march inland. He overcame the native Tlaxcalans and then formed an alliance with them against the Aztecs, their enemies. From that time until the conquest was achieved, the Tlaxcalans continued to be the most important of all the native allies of the Spaniards.

Montezuma pursued an irresolute policy during Cortés's march, and finally determined not to oppose the Spanish invaders but to await their arrival at the Aztec capital and to learn more about their purposes. On November 8, 1519, Cortés and his small force, with some 600 native allies, entered the city and established headquarters in one of its large communal dwellings. Some accounts say that the Aztecs may have believed Cortés was Quetzalcoatl, a legendary god-king who was light-skinned and bearded and, according to a prophecy, was expected to return from the east. The Spanish soldiers were allowed to roam through the city at their pleasure and found much gold and other treasures in the storehouses. Despite the amicable reception given the Spaniards, Cortés had reason to believe that attempts would be made to drive him out. To safeguard his position, he seized Montezuma as hostage and forced him to swear allegiance to Charles I, King of Spain, and to provide a ransom of an enormous sum in gold and jewels. Meanwhile Velázquez dispatched an expedition under the Spanish soldier Pánfilo de Narváez to Mexico. In April 1520, Cortés received word that Narváez had arrived on the coast. Leaving 200 men at Tenochtitlán under the command of Pedro de Alvarado, an explorer who had also been with Grijalva, Cortés marched with a small force to the coast, entered the Spanish camp at night, captured Narváez, and induced the majority of the Spaniards to join his force.

Meanwhile harsh rules by Alvarado had aroused the Aztecs in the capital. An Aztec revolt against the Spaniards and their own imprisoned ruler, Montezuma, was under way when Cortés returned to the city. He was allowed to enter with his followers and to join Alvarado, but thereupon was immediately surrounded and attacked. At Cortés's request, Montezuma addressed the Aztecs in an attempt to quell the revolt. The Aztec ruler was stoned, and he died three days later. The Spanish and their allies were driven out of the city by a group of Aztecs on a dark, rainy night, the famous Noche Triste ("Sad Night"), June 30, 1520. The Aztecs pursued the retreating Spanish troops. On July 7, 1520, after defeating a very large force of Aztecs, Cortés finally reached Tlaxcala. There, during the summer, he reorganized his army with the aid of some reinforcements and equipment from Vera Cruz. Cortés then began his return to the capital, capturing outlying Aztec outposts on the way. On August 13, 1521, after a desperate siege of three months, Cuauhtémoc, the new emperor, was captured, and Tenochtitlán fell.

Cortés built Mexico City on the ruins of Tenochtitlán. Colonists were brought over from Spain, and the city became the principal European city in America. Cortés consolidated control over Mexico, inflicting great cruelty on the indigenous peoples. The popularity that Cortés achieved in Spain because of his conquests and the riches he had sent resulted in his being named governor and captain general of New Spain in 1523. Cortés then undertook an expedition to Honduras from 1524 to 1526. Meanwhile, fearing his ambition, the Spanish court had sent officials to Mexico to investigate his acts. In 1528 Cortés was ordered to relinquish the government of Mexico and return to Spain. There he appealed to the king, was made marquis of the Valley of Oaxaca in southern Mexico, and was reappointed captain general. He was not restored, however, to the civil governorship of Mexico. Cortés married the daughter of the count of Aguilar and in 1530 returned to Mexico. There he found himself constantly checked in his activity, his property kept from him, his rights interfered with, and his popularity waning.

In 1536 Cortés discovered the peninsula of Baja California in northwest Mexico, and explored the Pacific coast of Mexico. In 1539 the Spanish explorer Francisco Vásquez de Coronado secured the right to seek the Seven Cities of Cíbola, and in disgust Cortés went back to Spain to complain to the court. Again he was received with honour but could secure no substantial assistance toward recovering his rights or his property. He served as a volunteer in 1541 in the unsuccessful Spanish expedition against Algiers, lost a large part of his remaining fortune, and was shipwrecked. Cortés, neglected by the court after the Algiers expedition, retired to a small estate near Seville, where he lived until his death.

## 12. Pän lo de Narväez

Pánfilo de Narváez (1470-1528), Spanish soldier and explorer. He assisted Diego Velázquez in the conquest of Cuba (1511). In 1520 he was sent to Mexico to subdue Hernán Cortés. The mission failed and Narváez was captured. After his release in 1521 he returned to Spain. In 1526 he was granted a patent by Charles V to conquer and settle Florida. He sailed in 1527 and landed on Florida's west coast near Tampa Bay. Sending his ships on to Mexico, he marched inland, but his forces suffered from attacks by Native Americans and lack of food. The survivors built crude boats and sailed along the Gulf Coast, where, off southern Texas, Narváez was washed out to sea in a storm.

## 13. Francisco de Orellana

Francisco de Orellana (1500-45), Spanish explorer and soldier, navigator of the Amazon river, born in Trujillo. He went to Peru in 1535. In 1540 he accompanied the Spanish explorer Gonzalo Pizarro as second-in-command on an expedition across the Andes Mountains into the country to the east, which was reported to abound in gold, silver, and cinnamon.

After a number of misfortunes the expedition reached the Napo River. When the supplies were exhausted, Orellana was ordered (1541) to sail down the Napo River with 50 men to search for provisions and signs of treasure. He descended the stream to its junction with the Amazon river, in present-day northeastern Peru; instead of returning, he proceeded down the river to the Atlantic Ocean. The voyage to the mouth of the Amazon lasted nearly eight months. From the mouth of the river he sailed back to Spain. His description of a marvelous race of female warriors, whom he named after the Amazons of Greek mythology, gave the river its name. Orellana was granted permission by the Spanish government to return and continue his exploits. In 1544 he set forth in a second expedition. He died in the new territory within a year.

## 14. Francisco Pizarro

Francisco Pizarro (1476-1541), Spanish conqueror and governor of Peru (1532-1541). He was born in Trujillo, Spain.

Pizarro was raised in poverty and never learned to read and write. He left Spain for the West Indies in 1502 and lived on the island of Hispaniola. In 1509 he joined Alonso de Ojeda's expedition to Colombia. Serving under Vasco Núñez de Balboa in 1513, he was his chief lieutenant when Balboa sighted the Pacific Ocean and claimed it for Spain. Later Pizarro served in Panama under governor Pedrarias Dávila, who had Pizarro arrest Balboa for treason. Balboa was then tried and quickly executed in January 1519.

In Panama, Pizarro heard tales of a southern land rich in gold. During the 1520s Pizarro led two expeditions down the west coast of South America and saw the golden ornaments worn by Native Americans of the Inca Empire of Peru. Returning to Spain, he secured the king's permission to conquer the land and become its governor.

Pizarro raised an army and returned to Peru in 1532. Atahualpa, the Inca, or emperor, quickly learned of the Spaniards' arrival but let them pass freely, awaiting them at the inland town of Cajamarca. When Pizarro reached Cajamarca, he invited the Inca and his nobles to a feast in the public square. On November 16, 1532, Atahualpa and thousands of nobles and soldiers came to meet the visitors, whom they called "children of the sun" because they believed they might be gods. Pizarro's troops, who numbered fewer than 200, then rushed forward brandishing their swords. They surrounded the startled and unarmed guests and, with the aid of horses and cannons, cut down almost all the leaders of the empire within half an hour. Atahualpa was captured alive and held for ransom. The emperor offered to fill a large room with gold, and two smaller rooms with silver, in exchange for his release. Pizarro agreed. Couriers came from all parts of the empire to fill the rooms with a treasure worth $100 million in today's money. After amassing this fortune, Pizarro broke his word and had Atahualpa executed on August 29, 1533.

Pizarro then marched south and took the Inca capital at Cuzco. After looting Cuzco he established the encomienda, or forced labor, system over the native people. With most of their leaders dead, they offered only sporadic resistance to Pizarro's rule. Pizarro governed Peru from Lima, which he founded in 1535.

The Spaniards then quarreled among themselves. Diego de Almagro, Pizarro's former partner who had been granted what is now northern Chile, claimed Cuzco and seized it. The power struggle between Pizarro and Almagro led to the War of Las Salinas in 1538. Almagro was killed, but his son, known as Almagro the Lad, continued the war. Pizarro was murdered in his palace in Lima by followers of Almagro in 1541.

# 15. Juan Ponce de Leön

Juan Ponce de León (1460-1521), Spanish explorer, born in San Servos, León. In 1493 he accompanied Christopher Columbus on his second voyage to America. Later Ponce de León conquered Borinquén (Puerto Rico) for Spain and was governor of the island from 1510 to 1512. From the Native Americans he heard tales of an island called Bimini, located somewhere north of Cuba, which reputedly possessed the fountain of youth, a spring whose waters had the power to restore youth. Believing these tales, Ponce de León in 1512 obtained permission from the Spanish king to find, conquer, and colonize Bimini. The next year Ponce de León sailed from Puerto Rico at the head of an exploratory expedition. On March 27 he sighted the eastern shore of the present state of Florida, which he believed to be the legendary Bimini. He landed north of the site of present-day Saint Augustine on April 2 and named the region Florida because he sighted it on Easter Sunday (Spanish Pascua Florida, "flowery Easter"). Believing Florida was an island, he tried to sail around it, going south to what is now Key West, up the west coast of Florida, then south again. He reached Puerto Rico again in September 1513. From 1515 to 1521 he engaged in subduing the rebellious natives of that island. In 1521 he set out to colonize Florida; the expedition included about 200 people and many domestic animals. The party landed on the west coast of Florida, where it was fiercely attacked by Native Americans. Ponce de León was severely wounded in the engagement. The expedition withdrew and sailed to Cuba, where he died shortly after landing.

## 16. Sebastiän Vizcaïno

Sebastián Vizcaíno (1550-1615), Spanish explorer, born in Huelva. After some time in Mexico, he headed expeditions to Lower California in 1596. He explored and carefully surveyed (1602-1603) the Pacific Coast north of Cape Mendocino; discovered a bay, which he named Monterey in honour of the Spanish administrator Gaspar de Zúñiga y Azevedo, count of Monterey; and dispatched a vessel northward from Cape Blanco, located on the southwest coast of the present state of Oregon. The vessel reached the mouth of a large river, probably the Columbia River, at the northern tip of Oregon.

Vizcaíno sailed (1611-1614) to East Asia, bringing missionaries from Spain to the Philippines and trying unsuccessfully to establish trade with Japan. His reports on his two voyages to California were published by the Spanish historian Juan de Torquemada in Monarquía Indiana (3 volumes, 1615); these reports, together with accounts of Vizcaíno's voyage to the Orient, also appear in Collection of *Voyages to The South Sea* (1811), compiled by the British historian James Burney.

## 17. Juan de Oôate

Juan de Oñate (circa 1550-c. 1630), Spanish-American explorer and administrator, founder of New Mexico (1598). Born in New Spain (now Mexico) he was related by marriage to Hernán Cortés and to the Aztec ruler Montezuma II. In 1595 he became governor of New Mexico, an unexplored region. In 1598, with 400 settlers, he founded San Juan de los Caballeros, near present-day Santa Fe. He subsequently led two fruitless searches for gold, one as far as modern Kansas (1601) and the other to the Gulf of California (1605). Relieved as governor in 1609, Oñate later (1614) was convicted of misconduct in office.

# Famous
## Portuguese Explorers

## 1. Juan Rodrïguez Cabrillo

Juan Rodríguez Cabrillo was a Portuguese explorer that is best-known for his 16th century discoveries in the Gulf of Mexico, most notably the coast of California.

Although information of his early life was not preserved, it is thought that he was born in 1499 in Portugal as the son of a shipbuilder. His first voyages happened in late 1520s as a crewmember of a Hernán Cortés that will become known in later years as the richest and most famous of the Mexican conquistadors. In 1539 he received orders form the Viceroy of New Spain (today's Mexico) of a new mission in which he will be tasked of exploring the newfound lands of Gulf of Mexico and finding a way to China (during that time navigators still presumed that the newfound lands were the part of the Asian continent). He embarked on that journey with three of his own ships on 27 June 1542 – San Miguel, La Victoria and his 200 tons flagship San Salvador. During that voyage he visited until then uncharted waters discovering San Diego bay, Santa Catalina island, San Clemente, San Pedro Bay and Point Conception. On his journey he missed the entrance of San Francisco Bay, which remained undiscovered for two more centuries since then.

On his return around Christmas of 1542, he entered into storm that damaged his ships, and few weeks later on 3 January 1543, he died from the wound that was infected by the gangrene.

His discoveries were not noticed during that time most notably because all of the expedition records were lost after his death. None of the names of the discovered lands were officially used but today he is still remembered as the first European that discovered the coast of California and as one of the founders of the Mexican city Oaxaca.

## 2. Pedro Álvares Cabral

Pedro Álvares Cabral was a Portuguese explorer, navigator and military commander who is best remembered today as the leader of the expedition that first reached that lands of South America that are today regarded as Brazil.

He was born in 1467 in the noble Portuguese family and was a member of a royal Portuguese court of King Manuel I and the King John II. On the turn of the century, King John II appointed Cabral with a mission to lead the 13-ship expedition to India following the route that Vasco de Gama discovered in 1497. Although he had navigation charts that contained the information of Vasco de Gama, Christopher Columbus and Bartolomeu Dias' journey he did not go directly to the India via the Cape of Good Hope. Instead, he went west and on April 23, he landed on the coast of Brazil. Believing that he discovered an island he named it Island of the True Cross and claimed it for the Portugal crown. After that, he resumed his trip to India losing four ships in a storm around west coast of Africa and three more on a later date, including the ship of the Bartolomeu Dias who first discovered Cape of Good Hope. Six remaining ships continued their journey but soon after that ship commanded by Diogo Dias become separated from the main fleet and they wandered alone following the east coast of Africa discovering the island of Madagascar.

On 13 September, he finally reached Calicut, India. There he negotiated the trade with current ruler of the city and even started to build factory and warehouse. That December however, he came under attack by the several hundred natives of that area and more than 50 Portuguese were killed. Outraged by this attack and the lack of explanation or apology from rule of Calicut he raided more than 10 local trade ships killing over 600 Indian sailors and bombarded the city with his cannons for an entire day.

After that massacre, he headed to the Indian city of Kochi where he managed to secure support of the local leaders and finally fill his ships with spices and other trade items from the east. On 16th of January 1501 he started his journey back to Europe where returned on 23rd of June.

Very soon after his return, King John II sent Amerigo Vespucci to a mission to explore this newfound land of South America. On that journey, Vespucci proved that South America was indeed part of a new continent and not just an island. In addition, a military fleet started forming with a mission to avenge Portugal's victims at the Calicut's attack but Pedro Álvares Cabral was not named as the expedition leader. In 1503, he married Isabel de Castro, and because of illness that he contained during the voyage, he remained in Portugal until his death in 1520.

Up to this day, it is not known why Cabral did not go straight to India, and instead went westward and discovered Brazil. Some speculations note that several other explorers visited lands very close to Brazil but historians claim that those journeys did not influence Cabral.

## 3. Diogo Céo

Diogo Cão was a Portuguese navigator and explorer best known for his exploits during the 15th century in a time known as Age of Discovery. He mapped the coast of the east Africa in his two voyages and founded several settlements in today's Angola.

He was born around 1450 in Vila Real, Portugal as an illegitimate son of a Royal house nobleman (Cão Alvaro Fernandes or Gonçalves Cão).

His first voyage started in 1482 just after the Portugal King John II established exploratory fleet with the purpose to navigate waters of lands between Europe and India and off course to Americas. Diogo Cão explored the African coast beyond the equator discovering the mouth of river Congo and Angola (Portuguese West Africa). His second journeys happened from 1484 to 1486 where Cão again visited African coast around equator up to Cape Cross in Namibia. He also sailed up the river of Congo.

Exact fate of Diogo Cão is not known. According to one source he died on River Congo, but there is speculation that he died during the journey back to Portugal.

# 4. Ferdinand Magellan

Ferdinand Magellan (1480 - 1521) was a Portuguese explorer that is best known for being the leader of a first successful mission to circumvent the Earth. He made that journey after he has obtained a Spanish nationality and started serving King Charles I of Spain.

Magellan was born around 1480 at Sabarosa, Portugal and from early age, he showed interest for the sea. At the age of 25, he started his sea life by joining the fleet of the Francisco de Almeida. Magellan continued sailing for the next 12 years until he managed to convince Spanish king Charles I to grant him the mission to find the "spice route" via the far lands of India via the lands that were discovered by Christopher Columbus. The fleet consisted of five ships (Trinidad, San Antonio, Concepción, Victoria and Santiago) and 237 crewmembers set their sails on 20 September 1519. During the first part of the journey they reached the coast of Argentine where they resupplied their food and soon after a small mutiny was squashed on two of the five ships. At November 1520, they travelled through the strait now known as the Strait of Magellan entering the waters of South Pacific.

They continued sailing to the west visiting the islands of Marianas, Guam and reaching the Philippines at Cebu. There he made contact with local leader Rajah Humabon and convinced him to convert to Christianity. Magellan was soon engulfed with a power struggle with hostile leader Datu Lapu-Lapu and on 27 April 1521, Magellan and much of his crewmembers were killed during one of battles with his forces. Rest of his crew (now travelling on only two ships – Trinidad and Victoria) led by the Spanish navigator Juan Sebastián Elcano continued on their way home travelling straight west from the Philippines directly to the Africa and Cape of Good Hope. During that route, Trinidad was in dire need of repairs and they lagged behind the Victoria. By then, Trinidad was captured by the Portugal, and in later years, only 15 Spanish crewmembers managed to find their way to Spain.

The last ship of the expedition Victoria continued on their way home, reaching the Spanish shores on 6 September 1522 with only 18 crewmembers aboard. The journey that lasted almost three years was not financially successful but its scientific discoveries were substantial – newfound lands, wildlife, and size of the Earth. In addition, their continuing journey to the west caused them to lose one day on a calendar. This discovery brought the invention of the International Date Line.

## 5. Bartolomeu Dias

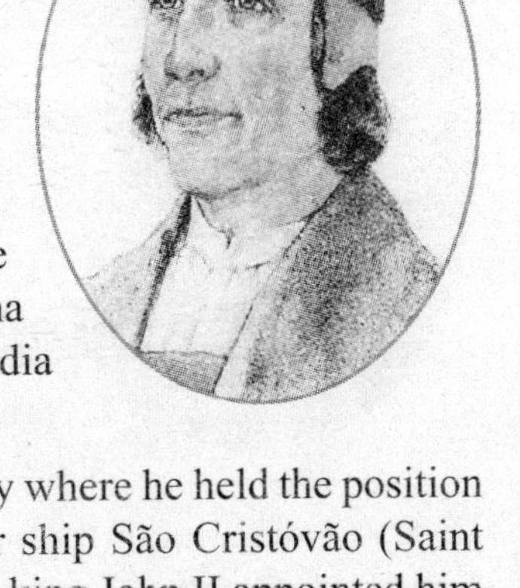

Bartolomeu Dias was a Portuguese explorer that is today best remembered for being the first European who sailed to the southern tip of Africa. His voyage opened the way for his compatriot Vasco da Gama who managed to find sea route to India in 1498.

Dias was born in 1451 in a royal family where he held the position of knight and sailing master of a war ship São Cristóvão (Saint Christopher). In late 1486, Portuguese king John II appointed him with a mission to explore the southern coast of Africa. In addition to finding the route to India, he was also tasked to visit the lands that were mentioned by Portugese explorer João Afonso de Aveiro (Ethiopia).

His journey south began in August 1487 with a fleet of three ships –São Cristóvão, São Pantaleão and support ship João de Santiago. After they replenished provisions at Sao Jorge de Mina, they reached the southern tip of Africa in March 12, 1488. One month later Dias discovered Cape of Good Hope (he named it "Cape of

Storms" before it was later renamed by King John II of Portugal), but his crew elected not to continue their journey further to east and India. After 16 months on the sea, Dias returned to Portugal bringing the news of a newfound route.

Next ten years he spent in the Portugal, planning his next mission and constructing several news ships. He joined Vasco da Gama on his journey to India, but he only sailed to Cape Verde Islands in the Atlantic. After that, Dias joined the expedition led by the Pedro Alvares Cabral where they discovered the coast of Brazil in 1500. Soon after, he died on a sea when four of his ships were sunk in a storm near the Cape of Good Hope. Shipwreck of his sunken fleet was never found.

## 6. Vasco da Gama

Vasco da Gama was a Portuguese governor and one of the best-known explorers in the time today known as "Age of Discovery". His most notable discovery happened during his 1497-1499 expedition where he successfully found sea route to India circumventing the African continent.

He was born around 1460s in Sines, Portugal as a son of Knight Estêvão da Gama. After the 1490's King John II of Portugal formed the exploratory fleet with a task to find the sea route to the distant India. In 1488, Bartolomeu Dias managed to reach the southern tip of Africa, opening the way for the new expeditions to the east. In the following years, Portugal explorers prepared themselves for the journey to India. New ships were constructed and additional maps were procured from the expeditions that visited India via the land trade route which was held (and heavily taxed) then by the Republic of Venice.

On 8 July 1497, Vasco da Gama started his journey to India travelling in a fleet of four ships led by his own flagship São Gabriel. During his travel, he visited the eastern shores of Africa and tried unsuccessfully to establish a trade deal with the Sultan of Mozambique. He arrived in India on 20 May 1498 but even there he did not manage to gain the trust of The King of Calicut. After filling his ships with valuable local merchandise, Gama started his journey back to Portugal. One year later, he finally managed to reach the Portugal coast with only two ships and 55 crewmembers.

At home, he was showered with praise, fame and fortune. King of Portugal named him "Admiral of the Indian Seas" and was awarded with rights to a land in Sines. Following that success, he sailed to the east two more times. In 1502, Gama commanded the fleet of fifteen ships to the coasts of east India where he was involved in several incidents against Arabs and Muslims, both on sea and on land. After bombarding city of Calcut he returned to Portugal in 1503 carrying full cargo of gold and silk.

In 1524, King of Portugal sent him to India to replace viceroy Eduardo de Menezes, but he died on a journey from malaria. Body of Vasco da Gama was initially buried in India, but he was returned to Portugal in 1539.

Although he never sailed in uncharted waters, never found unexplored land and his initial voyage route to India was greatly product of the knowledge of his Arab companion, Vasco da Gama's greatest historical success was kick starting the era of sea exploration in Spain and Portugal. After his journey, both of those countries dedicated much larger attention and resources to the exploration of the Indian route both to the east and to the west. Short time after Gama's journey to India several other explorers embarked on their famous journeys – Christopher Columbus to the West Indies, Pedro Álvares Cabral discovery of Brazil and Ferdinand Magellan's journey around the world.

# 7. Joéo de Castro

João de Castro (1500-1548), Portuguese naval officer and explorer, born in Lisbon. As a youth he distinguished himself in a number of campaigns against the Moors of Tangier and Tunis. In 1543, when he returned from an expedition to the Red Sea, he was appointed commander of a fleet to clear the European seas of pirates.

Castro was sent in 1545 to Portuguese India, where he overthrew the king of Gujarāt and relieved the beleaguered town of Diu. He subsequently completed the subjugation of Malacca and prepared the way for the invasion of Sri Lanka. In 1547 he was made viceroy of Portuguese India.

# Famous Italian Explorers

# 1. Eusebio Francisco Kino

Eusebio Francisco Kino (1645-1711), Italian explorer, cartographer, and missionary in southwestern North America, born in Segno. Educated in mathematics and astronomy at Jesuit schools in Italy and Germany, Kino (also spelled Chini, Chino, or Quino) became a member of the Society of Jesus in 1669. In 1681 he arrived in New Spain (now Mexico); in 1682 he published a pamphlet in Mexico City concerning his observations of a comet in Cádiz, Spain, in 1680.

Later in 1682, as mapmaker and Jesuit superior of an exploring and colonizing mission to Baja California, Kino began the work that was to occupy him for the rest of his life. In the region known as Pimería Alta, comprising what is now the southern part of Arizona and most of the Mexican state of Sonora, Kino spent nearly 30 years preparing maps, founding missions that eventually became towns and cities, and introducing agriculture and stock raising to the Native Americans. His maps, one of which first showed Baja California to be a peninsula rather than an island, remained standard for over a century.

## 2. Henri de Tonty

Henri de Tonty (1650?-1704), Italian explorer, born in Gaeta. As a youth he entered the service of France, and in 1678 he went with the French explorer René-Robert Cavelier, Sieur de La Salle, to Québec. He accompanied La Salle on his famous voyage down the Mississippi River in 1682 and was in command of Fort Saint Louis, in present-day Illinois, from the time of its erection until 1700, when he joined the Louisiana colony. An able administrator and successful colonist, he won the respect and admiration of the Native Americans. He was known as Iron Hand because of his artificial hand, a substitute for one he lost in battle while with the French army, and was believed by the Native Americans to have magical powers.

# 3. Amerigo Vespucci

Amerigo Vespucci was an Italian explorer, cartographer and navigator, best known for naming the North American continent with a slight variation of his first name and for proving the fact that New World is not part of an Asia but a new continent.

He was born in Florence, Italy in 1454 where he worked for the famous Medici family as a banker. In 1492, he moved to Spain, and few years later in 1458 king Manuel I of Portugal invited him to be part of a crew that will explore the Indian Ocean. Historical records of his journeys to the New World are not completely accurate, there is speculation of four but only two are completely verified.

On that journey under the leadership of Captain Alonso de Ojeda flotilla of ships separated in two parts, and Vespucci headed to the west toward the Brazil. There he discovered mouth of the great Amazon River. On a next expedition, he was elected to be a leader and they discovered that land of South America extended far more to the south than they have previously thought. On his way back, he passed near the rivers of Trinidad and Orinoco.

In 1501, he embarked on his last journey that was lead by the Portuguese explorer Gonçalo Coelho. Again, they explored the land of South America reaching the bay of Rio de Janeiro. During that time, he observed that Americas land size is way bigger than previous estimates and that these lands must be considered to be a fourth continent.

During his voyages, he mapped several charts of the nigh sky seen from the southern hemisphere, most notably constellation Southern Cross as well as the Alpha and Beta Centauri. Publication about his journeys released around 1503 made him very popular in Europe, and few years later German cartographer Martin Waldseemüller made a map of Vespucci's journeys in which for the first time he named the newfound continent America. Christopher Columbus wrote several times about Vespucci, and he never objected to the naming of the new continent.

Popularity of his journeys made him one of the most important explorers of that time and in 1508, King Ferdinand named him the chief navigator of Spain with the responsibility to coordinate and plan Spain's naval ship exploration of the Indies and the New World. He also founded first school of navigation with duties to standardize navigation techniques used by naval captains of that time.

He died in Spain on February 22, 1512 at the age of 57.

# 4. John Cabot

John Cabot (1450-1499), Italian navigator and explorer, who attempted to find a direct route to Asia. Although Cabot was probably born in Genoa, as a youth he moved to Venice, where his seafaring career probably began. He became a naturalized Venetian in 1476, but about eight years later settled in Bristol, England. Cabot had developed a theory that Asia might be reached by sailing westward. This theory appealed to several wealthy merchants of Bristol, who agreed to give him financial support. In 1493, when reports reached England that Christopher Columbus had made the westward passage to Asia, Cabot and his supporters began to make plans for a more direct crossing to the Orient. The proposed expedition was authorized on March 5, 1496, by King Henry VII of England.

With a crew of 18 men, Cabot sailed from Bristol on May 2, 1497, on the Matthew. He steered a generally northwestward course, and on June 24, after a rough voyage, he landed, perhaps on present-day Cape Breton Island; he subsequently sailed along the Labrador, Newfoundland, and New England coasts. Believing that he had reached northeastern Asia, he formally claimed the region for Henry VII. Cabot returned to England in August and was granted a pension. Assured of royal support, he immediately planned a second exploratory voyage that he hoped would bring him to Cipangu (Japan). The expedition, consisting of four or five ships and 300 men, left Bristol in May 1498. The fate of this expedition is uncertain. It is believed that in June, Cabot reached the eastern coast of Greenland and sailed northward along the coast until his crews mutinied because of the severe cold and forced him to turn southward. He may have cruised along the coast of North America to Chesapeake Bay at latitude 38° North. He was forced to return to England because of a lack of supplies, and he died soon afterward.

## 5. Christopher Columbus

Christopher Columbus was an Italian navigator and explorer that is today best remembered for being the first European to discover the New World. He made those discoveries with a funding provided by the Spanish King Ferdinand and Queen Isabella.

He was born in 1451 as an eldest son of a wool merchant Domenico Colombo. Even from the early ages, he travelled the seas, visiting Iceland in the age of 16. In the following years, he travelled the seas even engaging in the acts of Piracy, but in 1479, he settled in Lisbon where he started working as a cartographer. During that time, he tried several times to procure funding for his mission to find the Indies, but he was refused on multiple occasions by the Spain and France kings. Finally, in 1491 he gained the help of a priest Father Perez who managed to convince Spanish court of the potential gains of such discovery.

King Ferdinand and Queen Isabella finally agreed to a mission, giving him three ships and a crew of 120. On 8 September 1472, Columbus set sail with three ships The Santa Maria, The Nina and The Pinta. After a month, Columbus was almost stopped by a crew's mutiny but fate smiled on him and on October 12, he spotted land. On the same day, Columbus landed on a Watling's Island in the Bahamas naming it San Salvador. While still believing that he discovered India he continued exploring those waters finding Cuba and Hispaniola (Jamaica). There he established first Spanish settlement in the New Word before starting his return journey on 16 January 1492.

News of his discovery soon spread across Europe and on 25 September, he started his second journey to the New World, this time carrying about 1500 men on a fleet of 16 ships. He again visited Hispaniola and Haiti where he established another Spanish settlement. While searching for gold he encountered several hostile native tribes (Carib and Arawak).

Third journey of Columbus happened in 1498 with a goal of further exploring the sea beyond the Caribbean. His six ships sailed to Hispaniola and then went south and for the first time spotting the lands of South America. He explored Trinidad, mouth of Orinoco River, Tobago and Grenada.

During that time, Spanish heard rumours that Columbus and his brothers are planning to become rulers of newfound lands so they sent investigator Francisco de Bobadilla to bring him to justice. Without listening to any explanation, De Bobadilla imprisoned Columbus and brought in chains to Spanish court. There seeing their mistake Spanish King freed him and restored all of his ranks and properties.

On 11 May 1502, Christopher Columbus started his last journey with a fleet of six ships. His mission was to discover a Strait of Malacca that would lead him to the Indian Ocean. After visiting Hispaniola, he continued on west reaching the shores of Central America, mapping the Guanaja, Bay Islands, Honduras, Nicaragua,

Costa Rica and Panama. During that time, he heard from natives of a strait that connects Atlantic and a new vast ocean. During his return to Jamaica, he encountered storm that damaged all of his ships. We waited for more than a year for help to arrive from islands governor Nicolás de Ovando y Cáceres.

He died on 20 May 1506 in Spain, still convinced that he discovered the eastern lands of Asia.

# Famous French Explorers

# 1. Robert Cavelier de la Salle

Robert Cavelier de la Salle (1643-1687), French explorer in North America, who navigated the length of the Mississippi River and claimed the Louisiana region for France.

René-Robert Cavelier, Sieur de La Salle was born on November 22, 1643, in Rouen, France, and educated by the Jesuits. In 1666 he immigrated to Canada, was granted land on the St. Lawrence River, and became a trader. From 1669 to 1670 he explored the region south of Lakes Ontario and Erie, and he later claimed to have discovered the Ohio River in 1671. In the course of his explorations in the wilderness, La Salle became familiar with indigenous languages and traditions. Because of his capabilities, French colonial governor Louis de Buade, comte de Palluau et de Frontenac, appointed him commander of Fort Frontenac, then being built as a trading station. In 1674 La Salle was sent to France as Frontenac's representative to justify the building of the fort. His mission was successful, and he received a patent of nobility.

La Salle subsequently conceived a plan for exploring and trading farther west, and in 1677 he again visited France to secure royal approval of his scheme. He returned with Italian explorer Henri de Tonty, who became his associate. In 1679 he set out on a preliminary expedition, and after establishing forts at the mouth of the Saint Joseph River and along the Illinois River, in February 1680, he sent a group to explore the upper Mississippi River. La Salle then returned to Fort Frontenac to procure new supplies and funds. By spring he was able to travel west again, and he and Tonty proceeded with their party of French and indigenous peoples to the Mississippi, which they descended to the Gulf of Mexico in 1682, claiming all the land drained by the river for Louis XIV, king of France, and naming the region Louisiana. La Salle subsequently commenced construction of forts in the new territory. When Frontenac was recalled to France later in 1682, however, La Salle's rivals succeeded in turning the new governor against him.

Journeying to France in 1683, La Salle made a successful appeal to the king, who commended him for his discoveries and named him viceroy of North America. In 1684 he sailed from France with a fleet of four ships on an expedition to establish a colony at the mouth of the Mississippi River. When he reached the Gulf of Mexico he was unable to find the Mississippi, and landed on the shore of what is now Matagorda Bay, Texas, believing the bay to be the western outlet of the Mississippi. After several fruitless searches by land for the mouth of the river, La Salle realized his mistake. In January 1687 La Salle set out for Canada with a party of 17 men to procure help for the few members left of the original expedition. His men mutinied, however, and he was killed near the Trinity River. One of La Salle's supply ships, the Belle, sank in 1686 during a storm and was discovered in Matagorda Bay in 1995.

## 2. Pierre de Monts

Pierre de Monts (1560-1630), French explorer and colonizer in North America. A Huguenot who had served under Henry IV of France, de Monts was granted a trade monopoly in New France (France's colonial empire in North America) in 1603. In 1603 de Monts and French explorer Samuel de Champlain made an expedition to the St. Lawrence River. In 1604 the explorers established a colony on an island at the mouth of the Saint Croix River, between present-day Maine and New Brunswick; in 1605 they relocated the colony to Port Royal (present-day Annapolis Royal) in Nova Scotia. De Monts and Champlain used the colony as a base for exploring the east coast of North America.

## 3. Pierre Esprit Radisson

Pierre Esprit Radisson (1636-1710), French fur trader and explorer, whose trading expeditions led to the organization of the Hudson's Bay Company in 1670. Radisson settled in Canada in 1651; the following year he was captured and held by the

Iroquois until 1653. He and his brother-in-law, Médard Chouart, Sieur des Groseilliers, were the first Europeans known to have explored the area of Minnesota. They reached that area in 1659 on a search for an inland Northwest Passage while operating as coureurs de bois (unlicensed fur traders). On their return from that journey, the French government of Canada confiscated their cargo of furs because they had acquired it without a license. This made them unhappy with the French, and they went to England to seek backing for further ventures. The English organized the Hudson's Bay Company to trade for furs on Hudson Bay, and Radisson served the company as a guide and advisor. He founded Fort Nelson, the first permanent European settlement in what is now the province of Manitoba. After retiring from the Hudson's Bay Company, Radisson eventually settled in England in 1687. His journals were first published in 1885 as the Voyages of Peter Esprit Radisson.

## 4. Ëtienne Brúlë

Étienne Brûlé (1592-1632), French explorer, born in Champigny-sur-Marne. Brûlé was a member of the expedition led by the French explorer Samuel de Champlain in 1608 that resulted in the founding of Québec, Canada. In 1610 Champlain sent Brûlé to live among the Huron. Brûlé learned their language and served Champlain as an interpreter. In 1615 he was a member of Champlain's expedition that explored Lake Huron and Lake Ontario. The following year Brûlé was captured and tortured by the Iroquois.

Brûlé's later explorations are difficult to trace, but it is known that he explored the Susquehanna River as far as the Chesapeake Bay, and he is believed to have been the first European to see most of the Great Lakes. From about 1618 to 1629 Brûlé lived among the

Huron people, while he collected furs for the French. He turned against the French in 1629 and served as pilot on the St. Lawrence River for the British naval expedition that captured Québec and took Champlain prisoner. Brûlé returned to the Great Lakes to live with the Hurons, but was killed by hostile indigenous peoples.

## 5. Jacques Cartier

Jacques Cartier (1491-1557), French explorer and mariner, discoverer of the St. Lawrence River, born in Saint-Malo. Selected by King Francis I of France to lead an expedition to discover the Northwest Passage to China, he departed from St. Malo with two ships in April 1534. He sighted Newfoundland after 20 days, and sailing through the Strait of Belle Isle, between Newfoundland and Labrador, he proceeded southward along the western coast of Newfoundland and rounded the entire Gulf of St. Lawrence. On this voyage he saw Prince Edward Island and the New Brunswick mainland, sailed into Chaleur Bay (Baie des Chaleurs), which he named, landed on the Gaspé Peninsula, and crossed the St. Lawrence River estuary. Much of the French claim to Canada is based on Cartier's explorations.

Again sailing on orders from King Francis in 1535, Cartier crossed Belle Isle for the second time and then sailed up the St. Lawrence River, which he named on this occasion, as far as the indigenous village of Stadacona, where modern Québec stands. He later proceeded up the river to the indigenous village of Hochelaga and climbed the hill behind the village to observe the Ottawa River and Lachine Rapids. Cartier called the hill Mont Réal (Mount Royal), from which the name of the city of Montréal is derived. After spending the winter in Stadacona, Cartier sailed for France on a course south of Newfoundland, and for the first time passed through what is now called Cabot Strait.

Beginning his third voyage in 1541, Cartier again sailed up the St. Lawrence, this time as far as Lachine Rapids. His purpose was to establish a colony in Canada, but the mission was not successful. He returned to France the following year. He settled in St. Malo and wrote an account of his expeditions that was published in 1545.

## 6. Jean-Baptiste Le Moyne de Bienville

Jean-Baptiste Le Moyne de Bienville (1680-1768), French-Canadian explorer and colonial administrator, founder of Biloxi, Mississippi and Mobile, Alabama. Bienville was born in what is now Montréal, Québec, a member of a notable family of French explorers. In 1699, with his brother Pierre Le Moyne, Sieur d'Iberville, he founded a settlement called Old Biloxi in the French colony of Louisiana. The settlement was across Biloxi Bay from the present-day city of Biloxi, Mississippi. About 1700 Bienville explored the lower Mississippi River valley and the Red River region of what is now northeastern Texas. In 1702 he assumed leadership of the Louisiana colony and moved the colonial government from Old Biloxi to Fort Louis, on the Mobile River. Flooding of the river in 1711 caused Bienville to relocate the settlement 43 km (27 mi) south to the present-day site of Mobile, Alabama. He explored the Alabama River in 1714 and founded Fort Rosalie at what is now Natchez, Mississippi, in 1716.

In 1711 the French soldier Antoine de La Mothe, Sieur de Cadillac was officially appointed governor of the Louisiana colony. He arrived at the post in 1713. Bienville served as his second in command until 1716, when Cadillac returned to France and Bienville replaced him. In 1718, realizing its strategic importance, he laid out the city of New Orleans, which became the capital in 1722. His enemies accused him of incompetence, however, and in 1726 he was recalled to France and deprived of his office. Reinstated in 1732, Bienville again served as governor of Louisiana from 1733 to 1743, when he retired and returned to France.

## 7. Samuel de Champlain

Samuel de Champlain , 1567-1635, French explorer, the chief founder of New France.

After serving in France under Henry of Navarre (King Henry IV) in the religious wars, Champlain was given command of a Spanish fleet sailing to the West Indies, Mexico, and the Isthmus of Panama. He described this three-year tour to the French king in Bref Discours (1859). In 1603 he made his first voyage to New France as a member of a fur-trading expedition. He explored the St. Lawrence River as far as the rapids at Lachine and described his voyage in Des Sauvages (1603).

With the sieur de Monts , who had a monopoly of the trade of the region, Champlain returned in 1604 to found a colony, which was landed at the mouth of the St. Croix River. In 1605 the colony moved across the Bay of Fundy to Port Royal (now Annapolis Royal, N.S.), and in the next three years Champlain explored the New England coast south to Martha's Vineyard, discovering Mt. Desert Island and most of the larger rivers of Maine and making the first detailed charts of the coast. After the sieur de Monts's privileges had been revoked, the colony had to be abandoned, and through the efforts of Champlain a new one was established on the St. Lawrence River.

In 1608 in the ship Le Don de Dieu, he brought his colonists to the site of Quebec. In the spring of 1609, accompanying a war party of Huron against the Iroquois, Champlain discovered the lake that bears his name, and near Crown Point, N.Y., the Iroquois were met and routed by French troops. The incident is believed to be largely responsible for the later hatred of the French by the Iroquois.

In 1612 Champlain returned to France, where he received a new grant of the fur-trade monopoly. Returning in 1613, he set off on a journey to the western lakes. He reached only Allumette Island in the Ottawa River that year, but in 1615 he went with Étienne Brulé and a party of Huron to Georgian Bay on Lake Huron, returning southeastward by way of Lake Ontario. Accompanying another Huron war party to an attack on an Onondaga village in present-day New York, Champlain was wounded and forced to spend the winter with the Huron.

Thereafter Champlain devoted his time to the welfare of the colony, of which he was the virtual governor. He helped to persuade Richelieu to find the Company of One Hundred Associates, which was to take over the interests of the colony. In 1629 Quebec was suddenly captured by the English, and Champlain was carried away to four years of exile in England; there he prepared the third edition of his Voyages de la Nouvelle France (1632). When New France was restored to France in 1632, Champlain returned. In 1634 he sent Jean Nicolet into the West, thus extending the French explorations and claims as far as Wisconsin. He died on Christmas Day, 1635, and was buried in Quebec.

# 8. Sieur des Groseilliers

Sieur des Groseilliers (1618-1696), French fur trader and explorer of the territory around the northern Great Lakes and the Hudson Bay in Canada. He was born in the Marne region of northern France. He arrived in French Canada about 1639 and later acquired a land grant on the St. Lawrence River from which he derived his title, Sieur des Groseilliers. During his first few years in New France (as the French colony in North America was known), Groseilliers worked as an assistant to the Jesuit missionaries on the eastern shore of Lake Huron. In 1654 he embarked on his first fur-trading expedition, travelling by canoe from Québec up the St. Lawrence and Ottawa rivers to Lake Huron and through the Mackinac Straits into Lake Michigan. He established a trading post near present-day Green Bay, Wisconsin, and from there explored the Fox and Wisconsin rivers and the upper reaches of the Mississippi River.

Groseilliers returned to Québec in 1656, and three years later he joined his brother-in-law Pierre Esprit Radisson on another fur-trading expedition, this time to the western end of Lake Superior. From local indigenous people, Groseilliers learned of a river that reportedly flowed northward toward a "great sea." Groseilliers speculated that this might be a water route between the Great Lakes and Hudson Bay or even the long-sought Northwest Passage between the Atlantic and Pacific oceans. Although they did not discover such a route, Groseilliers and Radisson explored lands that were prime hunting grounds for fur traders, and they amassed a valuable cargo of furs. When the men returned to Montréal in 1660, French authorities accused them of engaging in unlicensed fur trading. They soon left French Canada, first for Boston, then for London, England, where they sought support for a large-scale fur-trading venture to Hudson Bay.

In 1667 a group of London merchants agreed to sponsor their fur-trading venture. The following year, Groseilliers sailed to James Bay, at the southern end of Hudson Bay, and established Fort Charles, which became the first permanent white settlement on the bay. The enterprise proved to be a success from the start, and two years later, in 1670, King Charles II of England granted a royal charter establishing the Hudson's Bay Company. For the next several years, Groseilliers worked for the company, which was given a trade monopoly over all the lands whose rivers emptied into Hudson Bay, a massive area comprising nearly half of what is now Canada. Groseilliers retired to his estate near Québec in 1684.

## 9. Louis Hennepin

Louis Hennepin (1626-1705), Flemish Recollect friar and explorer in North America, first European to explore the upper Mississippi River.

Hennepin was born in Ath (now in Belgium) on May 12, 1626. He travelled to Québec in 1675, where, for the next two years, he worked as a missionary among the Iroquois peoples. In 1678 he accompanied the French explorer René-Robert Cavelier, Sieur de La Salle, on an expedition through the Great Lakes to the Illinois River, on the banks of which they built Fort Crèvecoeur, near the site of present-day Peoria. From there Hennepin was sent by La Salle on a voyage to explore the upper Mississippi River, which he did by canoe. Hennepin explored and named the Falls of Saint Anthony (present-day Minneapolis, Minnesota). Proceeding further, he was captured by the Sioux, with whom he lived until his rescue the following year by a French exploring party from the Lake Superior region. After returning to France (1683),

Father Hennepin published *A Description of Louisiana* (1683; trans. 1938), an account of his travels, which was later exposed as plagiarism of La Salle's own accounts. For offering La Salle's narrative as his own and for claiming to have discovered the mouth of the Mississippi, Hennepin was exiled from France. He later wrote *A New Voyage* (1696; trans. 1698) and *A New Discovery of a Vast Country in America* (1697; trans. 1698).

# Famous
# Norwegian Explorers

## 1. Fridtjof Nansen

Fridtjof Nansen (1861-1930), Norwegian explorer, scientist, statesman, author, and Nobel laureate.

Nansen was born in Store Froën. He explored Greenland in 1882 and again in 1888, recording his experiences in *The First Crossing of Greenland* (1890) and *Eskimo Life* (1891). From 1893 to 1896 Nansen engaged in exploration of the Arctic regions, attaining 86°14' N, the most northerly point reached up to that time. The ship he used during this expedition, called the

Fram, was specially constructed to withstand the great pressure of ice. He described this journey in *Farthest North* (1897) and *The Norwegian North Polar Expedition* (6 volumes, 1900-1906).

In 1905 Nansen took part in the movement that led to the peaceful separation of Norway and Sweden and served (1906-1908) as the first Norwegian minister to Britain. From 1910 to 1914 he engaged in various explorations in the North Atlantic Ocean, Arctic Ocean, and Siberia. In 1917 he headed a commission to the U.S. to arrange various commercial agreements and in 1918 was a delegate to the Assembly of the League of Nations. He arranged for the repatriation of war prisoners in 1920, and from 1921 to 1923 he had general charge of the Red Cross famine relief in the Volga and South Ukraine regions of the USSR. For this latter work he received the Nobel Peace Prize in 1922. In 1927 he represented Norway on the disarmament committee of the League of Nations. The league honoured him by creating (1931) the Nansen International Office for Refugees, which won the 1938 Nobel Peace Prize.

Nansen wrote, in addition to works already mentioned, *The Oceanography of the North Polar Basin* (1902), *Through Siberia, the Land of the Future* (1914), *Spitzenbergen* (1922), and *Armenia and the Near East* (1928).

## 2. Roald Amundsen

Roald Amundsen was a Norwegian explorer best-known for his missions in the south and north Polar Regions. He was the first man to reach the South Pole and a first man to reach both Poles.

He was born on 6 July 1872 in Borge, Østfold, Norway as a fourth son of Jens Amundsen, respectable ship owner. At the age of 21, he started his life at the sea with a goal to live his life as an explorer. After an unsuccessful two year Antarctic mission led by the Adrien de Gerlache, he returned to Europe where he prepared for his first solo discovery. In 1903, he embarked on a mission to find the route trough the Northwestern Passage – small stretch of sea located between Arctic and Northern Canada that was previously unsuccessfully explored by several famous navigators John Cabot, Jacques Cartier, Henry Hudson, and James Cook. Travelling on a ship named Gjøa with six crewmembers, he successfully travelled trough those frozen waters gaining the knowledge of the lands and survival skills of the Northern people.

In the following years Amundsen planed his mission to North Pole but when he found out that explorers Frederick Cook and Robert Peary have already reached it he turned his sights to the South Pole. In June 1910, he left Norway and 6 months later reached the continent of Antarctica establishing the camp in the Bay of Whales. He made two attempts to reach the South Pole. During the first, he encountered extreme cold weather that made him return to camp. Second attempt was made with a crew of 6 people, 4 sleds and 52 dogs, travailing on a route that was previously explored by explorer Ernest Shackleton. On 13 December 1911, Roald Amundsen successfully reached the South Pole, naming that land as King Haakon VII's Plateau. Only five weeks later English explorer Robert Falcon Scott would reach the Pole, just to tragically die from cold and starvation while returning to his base camp.

After that successful feat, Amundsen went on a mission (1918-1925) to explore the waters of the Northwestern Passage. During that time, he collected great amounts of significant scientific data, and become interested in airplanes. He tried several times to flow over Arctic by air, a feat that was successfully made in 1926 when he and crew of 15 flew over the North Pole in a specially designed aircraft called Norge. Amundsen's aerial expedition was a fourth one that claimed success in reaching the North Pole (other three were on foot made by Frederick Cook in 1908, Robert Peary in 1909, and Richard Evelyn Byrd in 1926) but his was the only one that contained verified proof of their exact route.

Roald Amundsen died on June 18, 1928 while flying on a rescue mission in search of a missing plane. His body was never found.

## 3. Erik the Red

Erik the Red (lived about 950-1001), Norwegian explorer, the first European to explore Greenland and to find a colony there. He is also known as Eric the Red, Eirik the Red, and Eirik Thorvaldson. His second son, Leif Eriksson, is believed to have been one of the first Europeans to reach North America.

Erik was called Erik the Red because of his red hair. When his father was exiled for manslaughter, Erik left Norway with him, and the family settled in Iceland. In 980-981, faced with manslaughter charges himself, Erik decided to explore land sighted by his friend Gunnbjörn Úlfsson to the west of Iceland. The course Erik followed took him to the island he named Greenland. Returning to Iceland, he persuaded several shiploads of relatives and friends to join him in colonizing the new land in about 985. Because the eastern coast was sheathed in ice, he rounded Cape Farewell in the south and founded a settlement called Brattahlid. Others of his party established another settlement near present-day Nuuk (Godthåb). Both communities were on the western coast.

An injury prevented Erik from accompanying his son Leif on the voyage that eventually took him to Vinland (North America) in about 1001. He died the winter after Leif returned home. Another son, Thorvald, also visited Vinland.

# Famous American Explorers

## 1. Adolphus Washington Greely

Adolphus Washington Greely (1844-1935), American explorer of the Arctic and army officer.

Greely was born on March 27, 1844, in Newburyport, Massachusetts. After participating as a volunteer with the Union forces during the American Civil War, he entered the regular army in 1867. He was subsequently appointed to the signal service and from 1876 until 1879 supervised the erection of more than 3200 km (2000 mi) of telegraph line in Texas, the Dakotas, and Montana. In 1881 he became commander of an American expedition to establish one of a chain of 13 circumpolar meteorological stations recommended by the International Geographical Congress in 1879. His expedition discovered new territories north of Greenland, and several members of the group reached 83°24' north latitude, the northernmost point attained to that date. Relief parties sent out during 1882 and 1883 failed to reach the expedition, and during the winter of 1883 all the party except Greely and six of his men died. In the spring of 1884 survivors were rescued by U.S. Navy Commander Winfield Scott Schley. For his service in the Arctic, Greely was awarded the Founder's Medal of the Royal Geographical Society. In 1887 he was made chief signal officer and brigadier general, becoming the first volunteer and enlisted man in the U.S. Army to attain that rank. During the Spanish-American War he was in charge of constructing telegraph lines and establishing communications in Puerto Rico, China, Cuba, and the Philippines. He was later given a similar commission in Alaska, establishing the first wireless stations in the territory. Greely supervised relief operations in San Francisco after the 1906 earthquake. In that year he was promoted to major general, and two years later he retired from the army. He wrote Three Years of Arctic Service (2 volumes, 1885), Handbook of Alaska (1912), and The Polar Regions in the Twentieth Century (1928).

## 2. Charles Francis Hall

Charles Francis Hall (1821-1871), American explorer of the Arctic. He explored the southeast coast of Baffin Island (1860-1862), finding traces of the Inuit attack on the English navigator Martin Frobisher (1576-1578). Between 1864 and 1869, he travelled about 4830 km (about 3000 mi) by sledge and learned from the Inuit the fate of Sir John Franklin's expedition, lost in 1845. His own death in 1871, while attempting to reach the North Pole, stirred controversy in the 1960s, when an inquiry revealed sufficient traces of arsenic in his exhumed body to have caused his death.

## 3. Matthew A. Henson

Matthew A. Henson. (1866-1955), black explorer, member of the 1909 expedition led by American explorer Robert Peary that is generally credited with discovering the North Pole. Born in Charles County, Maryland, Henson ran away from home at age 11, after both parents had died. As a teen, he travelled the world for six years as a hand aboard the merchant vessel Katie Hines.

Henson was working as a hat store clerk in Washington, D.C., in 1897 when Peary hired him as a valet. Henson travelled with Peary on a survey expedition to Nicaragua in 1897 and accompanied him on seven polar expeditions. Henson quickly proved indispensable to Peary as a navigator in the Arctic and as a translator among the Inuit.

On April 6, 1909, an expedition made up of Peary, Henson, and four Inuit claimed to be the first to reach the North Pole. Henson, who usually broke trail while pulling a sled, may have reached the Pole 45 minutes before Peary, although discovery of the North Pole is usually credited to Peary. In recent years, however, most scholars have concluded that the point the expedition reached was actually at least a few miles from the North Pole.

In 1912, Henson wrote *A Black Explorer at the North Pole*. In 1913, President Taft personally recommended Henson's appointment to the United States Customs House in New York City in recognition of his exploits in the Arctic. In 1944 Henson received a joint medal from the Congress of the United States, honouring the Peary expedition to the North Pole. He was also honoured by President Truman in 1950 and admitted to the Explorer's Club, but he passed away in relative obscurity. In 1988, he was reburied in Arlington National Cemetery in Virginia with full honours.

## 4. James Bridger

James Bridger (1804-1881), American trader, explorer, and scout, born in Richmond, Virginia. He made numerous trapping and hunting expeditions in the northern Rocky Mountains region. In 1825, while travelling through Utah, Bridger explored Great Salt Lake, until then known only to the Native Americans. He served as a guide on several western exploratory expeditions, including one (1832-35) that was conducted by the American army officer Benjamin de Bonneville. In 1843 Bridger and Louis Vásquez founded Fort Bridger, Wyoming, and in 1856 he located what became known as Bridger's Pass, in central Wyoming. In 1859 and 1860 he visited the region that is now Yellowstone National Park. Until his descriptions of the geysers and other features of the region were verified, they were known as "Jim Bridger's lies."

# 5. Elisha Kent Kane

Elisha Kent Kane (1820-1857), American explorer, physician, and scientist, author of Arctic Explorations: *The Second Grinnel Expedition.* (2 volumes, 1856). He was born in Philadelphia, and educated at the universities of Virginia and Pennsylvania. In 1842 he became an assistant surgeon in the United States Navy. He served in 1850 with the U.S. Coast Survey as surgeon and naturalist in the first expedition sent to search for the party of the British explorer Sir John Franklin, who had been lost in the Arctic in 1845. In 1853 Kane was appointed head of an Arctic exploration party, in command of the Advance. He sailed through Baffin Bay and Smith Sound into the basin now bearing his name, and his expedition remained there for 21 months. The expedition explored as far as 80°35' north, farther than anyone had previously gone. When provisions ran low, Kane and his group abandoned the Advance and set out for the Danish settlements in Greenland, reaching Upernavik in August 1855 after a hazardous overland journey of three months. For his book Arctic Explorations: The Second Grinnel Expedition, Kane was awarded medals by the U.S. Congress and the Royal Geographical Society. Other writings include The U.S. Grinnel Expedition in Search of Sir John Franklin (1853).

# 6. John C. Frëmont

John C. Frémont (1813-1890), American explorer, army officer, and politician, noted for his explorations of the Far West.

John Charles Frémont was born on January 31, 1813, in Savannah, Georgia, and educated at the College of Charleston, South Carolina. In 1838 he was commissioned second lieutenant in the Corps of Engineers, U.S. Army. During the following year Frémont was a member of the expedition of the French explorer Joseph Nicolas Nicollet that surveyed and mapped the region between the upper Mississippi and Missouri rivers. Between 1842 and 1845 Frémont led three expeditions into Oregon Territory. During the first, in 1842, he mapped most of the Oregon Trail and ascended, in present-day Wyoming, the second highest peak in the Wind River Mountains, afterward called Fremont Peak (4185 m/13,730 ft). In 1843 he completed the survey of the Oregon Trail to the mouth of the Columbia River on the Pacific coast. The party, guided by the famous scout Kit Carson, turned south and then east, making a midwinter crossing of the Sierra Nevada Mountains. Frémont made his third expedition in 1845, further exploring both the area known as the Great Basin and the Pacific coast.

During the Mexican War (1846-1848), Frémont attained the rank of major and assisted greatly in the annexation of California. He was appointed civil governor of California by the U.S. Navy commodore Robert Field Stockton, but in a conflict of authority between Stockton and the U.S. Army brigadier general Stephen Watts Kearny, Frémont refused to obey Kearny's orders. He was arrested for mutiny and insubordination and was subsequently court-martialed. He resigned his commission after President James Polk remitted his sentence of dismissal from the service. In the winter of 1848 and 1849 Frémont led an expedition to locate passes for a proposed railway line from the upper Río Grande to California. In 1850 he was elected one of the first two senators from California, serving until 1851. In 1856 he was the presidential candidate of the newly formed Republican Party, but was defeated by James Buchanan. During the American Civil War Frémont was appointed a major general in the Union Army and held several important but brief commands; he resigned his commission in 1862 rather than serve under General John Pope. In 1864 Frémont was again a presidential nominee; he withdrew, however, in favour of President Abraham Lincoln. He served as governor of the territory of Arizona from 1878 to 1883. In 1890 he was restored to the rank of major general and retired with full pay. He died in New York City on July 13, 1890.

Frémont wrote Report of the *Exploring Expedition to the Rocky Mountains* in the Year 1842, and to *Oregon and North California* in the Years 1843-1844 (1845) and *Memories of My Life* (1887).

## 7. Donald Baxter MacMillan

Donald Baxter MacMillan (1874-1970), American explorer, born in Provincetown, Massachusetts, and educated at Bowdoin College and Harvard University. He first explored (1908-9) the Arctic in the North Polar Expedition, led by the American explorer Robert Edwin Peary. MacMillan made 27 trips to the polar regions during the next 45 years. He led expeditions in Greenland, Labrador, and Baffin, Ellesmere, and Axel Heiberg islands, and he preserved rare samples of arctic vegetation and mineral deposits. In 1925 he directed a polar expedition in Greenland with the aid of U.S. Navy commander Richard Evelyn Byrd. For his explorations and scientific researches, MacMillan received many awards, including the special congressional medal (1944) and the Hubbard Gold Medal (1953) of the National Geographic Society. His writings include Four Years in the White North (1918), Etah and Beyond (1927), and How Peary Reached the Pole (1932).

## 8. Louise Arner Boyd

Louise Arner Boyd (1887-1972), American explorer of the Arctic Ocean and the first woman to fly over the North Pole. Boyd was born to a wealthy family in San Rafael, California, a suburb of San Francisco. Boyd inherited her family's fortune in 1920 and spent the next few years travelling in Europe. Her interest in polar exploration began in 1924 when she first visited Arctic regions aboard a Norwegian cruise ship. Two years later Boyd chartered a Norwegian ship and took a group of friends on a trip from Norway into the Arctic Ocean. They visited Franz Josef Land, the island chain north of European Russia, where they hunted polar bears and seals.

In 1928 Boyd led an expedition to find Norwegian Arctic explorer Roald Amundsen, who had disappeared while flying a rescue mission in search of Italian explorer and engineer Umberto Nobile. Financing the venture herself, Boyd set out on behalf of the Norwegian government on a voyage across about 16,100 km (about 10,000 mi) of the Arctic Ocean, exploring from Franz Josef Land in the east to the Greenland Sea in the west. She was unable to find any trace of Amundsen, but for her efforts the Norwegian government awarded Boyd the Chevalier Cross of the Order of Saint Olav.

Beginning in 1931, Boyd undertook a series of nearly annual expeditions to the Arctic. That year she and an exploring party sailed to Greenland's northeastern coast, where they examined glacial formations and photographed Arctic plant and animal life. She earned recognition for her explorations of the little-known De Geer Glacier when an adjoining region was later named Louise Boyd Land. In 1933 Boyd led an expedition sponsored by the American Geographical Society. Her scientific team again studied the fjords and glaciers on Greenland's northeastern coast and, using a sonic device, measured the offshore ocean depths. In 1937, and again in 1938, Boyd continued her ocean-depth research in the Arctic seas northeast of Norway. These two expeditions helped determine that an undersea mountain ridge spans the ocean floor between Bear Island and Jan Mayen Island.

The outbreak of World War II in 1939 halted Boyd's explorations until 1941, when she undertook an Arctic expedition sponsored by the United States government. She studied the effects of polar magnetic phenomena on radio communications and later served as an adviser on military strategy in the Arctic. In 1949 the U.S. Army awarded her a Certificate of Appreciation in recognition for this work.

Boyd returned to the Arctic again in 1955 when, at the age of 68, she hired an airplane and became the first woman to fly over the North Pole. She spent her remaining years in San Francisco. Boyd wrote about her explorations in newspaper articles and in her books *The Fjord Region of East Greenland* (1935) and *The Coast of Northeast Greenland* (1948).

## 9. George Washington De Long

George Washington De Long (1844-81), U.S. explorer of the Arctic. In July 1879 he set out from San Francisco in an attempt to reach the North Pole. By September his ship was trapped in ice east of Wrangel Island. It then drifted for 21 months before being crushed and sinking. De Long and 13 of his crew died of cold and starvation, never reaching their destination, the Siberian coast, about 965 km (about 600 mi) away. Wreckage from the ship was found three years later on an ice floe off Greenland, supporting the theory of transarctic ice drift.

## 10. Lincoln Ellsworth

Lincoln Ellsworth (1880-1951), American explorer and engineer, and a leader of transarctic and transantarctic flights. He was born in Chicago on May 12, 1880.

Ellsworth organized and led (1924) a geological survey of the Andes Mountains from the Pacific Ocean to the headwaters of the Amazon River. He became an associate and financial supporter of the Norwegian explorer Roald Amundsen, and in May 1925 they and four companions attempted to fly over the North Pole. They took off from Svalbard in two amphibious airplanes but were forced to land just short of the pole. The following year, with the Italian explorer and engineer Umberto Nobile, Ellsworth and Amundsen carried out a 5460-km (3390-mi) flight in the dirigible Norge, from Kongsfjord, Svalbard, across the North Pole to Teller, Alaska. In November 1935 Ellsworth made the first airplane flight across the Antarctic from the Weddell Sea to the Ross Sea. He collaborated with Amundsen in writing *Our Polar Flight* (1925) and *First Crossing of the Polar Sea* (1927). Ellsworth also wrote *Search* (1932) and *Beyond Horizons* (1938). He died in New York City on May 26, 1951.

## 11. Robert Gray

Robert Gray (1755-1806), American explorer and sea captain, born in Tiverton, Rhode Island. During the American Revolution he served in the navy. In 1787 he sailed from Boston to the Pacific Northwest as commander of the Lady Washington, one of two ships on a fur-trading expedition subsidized by Boston merchants. After a load of furs was procured from coastal Native Americans, Gray was made head of the expedition and placed in command of the Columbia. He sailed to China and then westward, arriving in Boston on August 10, 1790, the first American to have circumnavigated the globe. A second voyage to the Pacific Northwest led to his discovery, in 1792, of the mouth of the Columbia River, which he named after his ship. He completed the trip around the world a second time, arriving in Boston in July 1793. The explorations and discoveries of Gray in the Pacific Northwest gave the United States a basis for claim to the Oregon country.

## 12. William Clark

William Clark (1770-1838), American explorer, Native American agent, and frontier politician, who served as co-leader, with Meriwether Lewis, of the Lewis and Clark Expedition (1804-1806), the first overland exploration of the American West and Pacific Northwest. Clark was born in Caroline County, Virginia. In 1784 the Clark family moved to the Kentucky frontier, establishing a plantation called Mulberry Hill near present-day Louisville.

Clark followed the powerful examples of his brothers Jonathan and George Rogers Clark, both of whom made military life the path to success. In 1789 William joined a militia company and soon became an infantry officer in the army of General Anthony Wayne. During service in the Indian wars in the Ohio Valley, Clark gained a reputation for leadership and courage. He met Meriwether Lewis at this time when Lewis served briefly in Clark's rifle company. Under General Wayne, Clark took part in the Battle of Fallen Timbers (near what is now Toledo, Ohio) in August 1794, which destroyed the power of the Native Americans in Ohio. Clark also grew to be an experienced frontier diplomat, earning Wayne's praise for a dangerous scouting mission in 1796. When debts incurred by George threatened Clark family lands in Kentucky and Indiana, William resigned his commission and spent the next eight years defending family interests.

In June 1803 Lewis asked Clark to join him as co-leader on a government-sponsored expedition through the Louisiana Territory to the Pacific Ocean. Clark was promised a captain's commission to match Lewis's rank, but bureaucratic confusion made him a lieutenant. Despite this, both Lewis and U.S. President Thomas Jefferson, who commissioned the expedition, always considered Clark an equal partner in command.

As commanding officers on the Lewis and Clark Expedition, Lewis and Clark informally divided leadership responsibilities. Clark was the expedition's mapmaker. Years of frontier experience had taught him to understand and record intricate terrain – land, rivers, and mountains. Clark's army experience also prepared him to be the expedition's most able negotiator and diplomat, a role he played in many meetings with Native Americans.

The expedition to the Pacific made Clark both famous and influential. For the rest of his life he played a key role as a federal Native American agent and territorial politician. In 1807 Clark was appointed agent for the tribes west of the Mississippi River.

During the War of 1812 (1812-1815) Clark worked to organize western defenses against British and Native American attacks. At the end of the war Clark and other federal officials negotiated a series of Native American treaties that reestablished American power in the West. As a Native American agent and governor of the Missouri Territory (1813-1821), Clark earned the respect of many native people who knew him as "the red-head chief."

After Lewis's death in 1809, Clark assumed responsibility for completing the report of the Lewis and Clark Expedition. Clark employed American financier and diplomat Nicholas Biddle to prepare the two-volume collection, finally published in 1814. The large map of the West that Clark drafted for the report is a landmark in the geographic understanding of the American West.

When Missouri became a state in 1821, Clark was defeated in his bid to become governor. Although his power in Native American affairs was much diminished, Clark continued to act on behalf of the federal government. At the time of his death, Clark had a national reputation as an authority on the West.

## 13. May French Sheldon

May French Sheldon (1847-1936), American explorer and best-selling author, who was one of the first white women to visit parts of eastern and central Africa. She was born in Beaver, Pennsylvania. After finishing school, she worked in the publishing business in London, England. In 1876 she married American businessman Eli Lemon Sheldon.

Inspired by the writings of her friend, Anglo-American explorer and journalist Sir Henry Morton Stanley, Sheldon set out for Mombasa, a city on the coast of present-day Kenya, in 1891. Financed by her husband, she was accompanied by more than 100 porters, servants, and guides. After British authorities in Mombasa refused to help with her travel plans, Sheldon went to nearby Zanzibar, where the sultan of Zanzibar gave her porters and a letter of safe conduct for her journey into the interior of what is now Tanzania. Sheldon first visited the area around Kilimanjaro, Africa's highest peak. Then, accompanied by a British official, she ventured into the surrounding territory and became one of the first white people to explore Lake Chala, which sits inside a steep volcanic cone. Sheldon next ascended about one-quarter of the way up Kilimanjaro to visit another settlement and meet with the local sultan. Her expedition was cut short when she suffered injuries in a fall. She received medical aid and then returned to Mombasa, where she sailed home to England. Sheldon wrote of her travels in *Sultan to Sultan* (1892), in which she described her contact with more than 35 different tribes of Central and East Africa. The book became a best seller in England and the United States.

Sheldon made her second trip to Africa in 1903, visiting the Belgian Congo (now the Democratic Republic of the Congo, DRC, formerly Zaire). During World War I (1914-1918), Sheldon raised money for the Belgian Red Cross by giving lectures on her travels in Africa. After the war the Belgian government honoured Sheldon by awarding her the Chevalier de l'Ordre de la Couronne.

## 14. Benjamin Louis Eulalie de Bonneville

Benjamin Bonneville (1796-1878), American explorer and soldier. Benjamin Louis Eulalie de Bonneville was born in Paris and brought to the United States by his parents. He graduated from the U.S. Military Academy in 1815 and entered the army. After gaining experience with the fur trade while serving at frontier posts,

Bonneville obtained a leave of absence from the army and in 1832 led an expedition into the Rocky Mountains. Making his base on the Green River in Wyoming, he spent the next four years in fur trading and exploring. Having overstayed his leave from the army, he was dismissed.

Soon after his return from the expedition in 1836 his journals were edited by the American author Washington Irving and published as *The Adventures of Captain Bonneville, U.S.A., in the Rocky Mountains and the Far West* (2 volumes, 1837). He was reinstated in the army in 1836 and served in the Mexican War. Bonneville retired in 1861 but reentered the army during the American Civil War and in 1865 was promoted to the rank of brigadier general. He retired again in 1866. The prehistoric Lake Bonneville, of which the Great Salt Lake in Utah is a remnant, is named in his honour.

## 15. Meriwether Lewis

Meriwether Lewis (1774-1809), American explorer who served as co-leader, with William Clark, of the Lewis and Clark Expedition (1804-1806), the first American overland exploration of the West and Pacific Northwest. Born in Albemarle County, outside Charlottesville, Virginia, Lewis grew up in Virginia and Georgia as part of the Southern planter aristocracy. During his education, Lewis showed special talent for natural history, which encompassed the modern fields of botany and zoology. Lewis proved to be a keen observer of the natural world, an attribute he put to use during the expedition.

Lewis joined the Virginia militia as a private soldier during the Whiskey Rebellion, a series of disturbances in 1794 aimed against the imposition of a federal excise tax on whiskey. Lewis soon became a junior officer, and he transferred to the regular army in 1795. As an officer in the First Infantry Regiment, Lewis served in the Indian wars of the Ohio Valley, where he briefly spent time in the rifle company of William Clark, the eventual co-leader of the Lewis and Clark Expedition.

Meriwether Lewis's life changed dramatically in 1801, when President Thomas Jefferson selected the young officer as his personal secretary. At first Lewis's secretarial duties were routine and administrative. But those responsibilities suddenly grew larger once Jefferson decided to send an expedition to the Pacific. By the end of December 1802 Lewis was preparing a preliminary estimate of travel expenses for the journey, and he began to purchase supplies and consult with scientists in the spring of 1803.

By June 1803, as Jefferson drafted formal expedition instructions for Lewis, it became clear that the expedition was going to be larger and more complex than originally planned. Jefferson and Lewis agreed that the party needed a co-leader. Lewis turned to William Clark. By early December 1803 the expedition party, now known as the Corps of Discovery, assembled at Wood River camp outside St. Louis. Lewis, commissioned a captain, and Clark, commissioned a lieutenant, divided their time during the winter of 1803 to 1804 between training duties and visits to St. Louis.

During the expedition to the Pacific and back, Lewis and Clark worked out an informal but effective division of responsibilities. Lewis served as the expedition's naturalist, making detailed notes about plants and animals new to European and United States science. He also represented Jefferson's aspirations for an expanding American empire in the West. It was this role that led to Lewis's involvement in the expedition's only violent encounter with Native Americans. In late July 1806, on the expedition's return journey, Lewis led a small exploring party into present-day north central Montana. While looking for the northern reaches of the Marias River and an American claim to fur-rich country, Lewis came upon a group of Piegan Blackfoot warriors. When the young Piegans attempted to take Lewis's horses and guns, violence erupted and two Native Americans were killed.

When the expedition returned to St. Louis in September 1806, Lewis and Clark became national heroes. President Jefferson appointed Lewis governor of the Louisiana Territory, an administrative post for which the explorer was ill-suited. In the years that followed, Lewis struggled with one complex political problem after another. He also worked on a formal report of the expedition, making little progress. Lewis's temperament during this period was marked by episodes of depression. Personal financial difficulties, political troubles, questions about his effectiveness as governor, and the long-delayed expedition report all weighed heavily on him. In September 1809 Lewis left St. Louis for Washington, D.C., to answer his critics. Sometime during the night of October 10 near Hohenwald, Tennessee, Lewis apparently took his own life. Despite claims by some that Lewis was murdered, all the surviving evidence points to suicide. Lewis left behind a remarkable legacy of knowledge about the American West. Clark and American diplomat and financier Nicholas Biddle eventually published an abridged, two-volume collection of the expedition's journals in 1814. A complete set of the journals was finally published in 1905.

## 16. John Muir

John Muir (1838-1914), American naturalist, explorer, and writer. He was an influential conservationist, who worked to preserve wilderness areas and wildlife from commercial exploitation and destruction. His efforts helped to establish Yosemite National Park and Sequoia National Park, both in California. Many natural sites have been named in his honour, including Muir Woods National Monument, a virgin stand of redwoods, near San Francisco, California.

Muir was born in Scotland in 1838. His family immigrated to the United States when he was 11 years old and settled on a farm near Portage, Wisconsin. Muir attended the University of Wisconsin from 1860 to 1863 but did not graduate. When he left college, he took extensive walking trips to study nature, especially plants. In 1867 he made a walking trip from Indianapolis to the Gulf of Mexico to observe the plants, animals, and physical features of the country. During this trip Muir kept extensive journals, which were published after his death as *A Thousand Mile Walk to the Gulf* (1916).

In 1868 Muir went to Yosemite Valley in California and explored and studied the area for the next six years. He was the first to conceive the theory that the Yosemite Valley was formed by glacial erosion. During this time he also studied glaciers in the Sierra Nevada Mountains. In 1879, while exploring Glacier Bay, Alaska, he sighted the glacier that now bears his name, the Muir Glacier.

In 1880 Muir married and settled on a fruit ranch in Martinez, California. During the next ten years, he became a noted and financially successful horticulturist. In 1891 he resumed his travels. He had become interested in the study of trees, especially pines and sequoias, and went to Australia, Africa, Europe, and South America to visit the forests. As a result of his studies, Muir became a strong proponent of the need to preserve nature for its own sake. He argued forcefully that people should defend species and wilderness areas from devastation by humans.

In 1889 he initiated a movement to preserve the sequoias in the Yosemite Valley and the surrounding area. In 1890 his efforts led Congress to establish Yosemite and Sequoia national parks. In 1892 Muir and some of his supporters founded the Sierra Club, dedicated to the exploration and preservation of American wildlife and wilderness. He also influenced President Theodore Roosevelt to set aside national monuments, national forest reserves, and national parks.

However, Roosevelt did not support Muir's efforts to block the building of the Hetch Hetchy Dam, a project designed to bring water from the Sierra Nevada Mountains to San Francisco. The proposed dam would flood the Hetch Hetchy Valley, in the northern part of Yosemite National Park. Muir passionately opposed the dam, arguing that flooding the valley would destroy a valuable natural area. His efforts, however, were not successful, and President Woodrow Wilson authorized the building of the dam in 1913. Muir died the next year.

In recognition of Muir's efforts as a conservationist and crusader for national parks, Muir Woods National Monument was established in 1908. Muir's home in Martinez, California, along with his gravesite and part of his fruit orchard, were designated the John Muir National Historic Site in 1964. Muir wrote many books and articles, including *The Mountains of California* (1894), *Our National Parks* (1901), *My First Summer in the Sierra* (1911), *The Yosemite* (1912), and *Travels in Alaska* (1915).

## 17. Zebulon Montgomery Pike

Zebulon Montgomery Pike (1779-1813), American explorer and soldier. He was born in Lamberton, New Jersey, and entered the United States Army about 1793. Pike was a lieutenant when in 1805 he was chosen by General James Wilkinson to find the headwaters of the Mississippi River. In the winter of 1805 and 1806 he reached Red Cedar Lake (now Cass Lake) and Leech Lake in Minnesota, erroneously believing them to be the Mississippi's source. The actual source, Lake Itasca, was determined in 1832. He also bought land from the Sioux people for the future site of Fort Snelling, which grew into the city of Minneapolis, Minnesota.

In July 1806 Wilkinson sent Pike to explore the headwaters of the Arkansas and Red rivers. Pike travelled up the Arkansas River into South Park, a tableland in the Southern Rocky Mountains in Colorado. He also explored the region south of what is now Leadville, Colorado, and sighted and attempted to climb Pikes Peak. From the Arkansas River he turned south, crossing the Sangre de Cristo Mountains into the Spanish territory of New Mexico. The Spanish arrested Pike and imprisoned him at Santa Fe, New Mexico, and Chihuahua, Mexico. He was released in 1807 and returned to the United States with valuable information about the geography of the Southwest. His report stimulated great interest in the settlement and trade of that region.

Pike was commissioned a brigadier general at the beginning of the War of 1812. He was killed by the explosion of a powder magazine, April 27, 1813, while leading American forces in an assault on the capital of Upper Canada, York (now Toronto, Ontario).

## 18. John Wesley Powell

John Wesley Powell (1834-1902), American ethnologist, geologist, explorer, and government administrator, known for his work as the first major classifier of Native American languages, as well as for his pioneering work as a geographical and geological surveyor of the Rocky Mountains.

Powell was born on March 24, 1834, at Mount Morris, New York. When his family moved to Illinois, he made long solo voyages on the Ohio and Mississippi rivers and became intensely interested in nature. After study at Oberlin and Wheaton colleges and service in the Union army during the American Civil War, he became a geology professor at Illinois Wesleyan College in 1865, and later he lectured at Illinois Normal University. In 1867 and 1868 he led geological expeditions into Colorado and Utah. The next year, with government backing, he explored and made a geological survey of the Green and Colorado river canyons. Between 1870 and 1879 he continued his survey of the Rocky Mountain region.

During Powell's travels he studied the Native Americans he encountered, and in 1879 he was appointed the first director of the U.S. Bureau of Ethnology. He also served (1881-92) as head of the U.S. Geological Survey, which under his direction became a highly effective organization. In 1891 he published the first complete classification and distribution map of the 58 language stocks of the Native Americans of the United States and Canada. He died in Haven, Maine, September 23, 1902.

Powell's books include *Explorations of the Colorado River of the West* (1875), *An Introduction to the Study of Indian Languages* (1877), and *Report on the Lands of the Arid Region of the United States* (1878).

## 19. Henry Rowe Schoolcraft

Henry Rowe Schoolcraft (1793-1864), American explorer and ethnologist, born in Watervliet, New York, and educated at Middlebury College in Vermont and at Union College (now Union College and University in Schenectady, New York). In 1817-18 he explored Missouri and Arkansas, gathering geological, geographical, and mineralogical information. He served as geologist on the expedition led by the American general Lewis Cass in 1820 that explored the Lake Superior region. From 1822 to 1836 Schoolcraft served as Native American agent for the tribes of that region and from 1836 to 1841 as superintendent of Indian affairs for Michigan. In 1832 he led the expedition that discovered the sources of the Mississippi River. Schoolcraft devoted much of his life to the study of the Native Americans and was one of the first to write about their culture. His most important work is the monumental study *Historical and Statistical Information Respecting the History, Condition,* and *Prospects of the Indian Tribes of the United States* (6 volumes, 1851-57).

## 20. Jedediah Smith

Jedediah Smith (1798-1831), American fur trapper and explorer. Jedediah Strong Smith was born in Bainbridge, New York. He became a fur trapper in the West as a young man and in the last six years of his life earned a place as one of the greatest pathfinders in American history. In 1826 he ventured southwest with a party of 17 from Great Salt Lake in search of trade routes (for fur-trapping rights) to California and the Northwest. After crossing the Mojave Desert, he reached Mission San Gabriel, California, near present-day Los Angeles, probably the first white to reach California from the East. Sent away by the Spanish governor, who was suspicious of Smith, he proceeded north, becoming the first American to cross the Sierra Nevada Mountains; proceeding northeast across present-day Nevada, he became the first white to cross the Great Salt Lake Desert. Upon returning (1827) to California, ten of his men were killed by Native Americans; in 1828 Native Americans killed most of his party on an expedition to Fort Vancouver (now Vancouver, Washington). Smith was later killed by the Comanche on the Santa Fe Trail.

## 21. Paul Belloni du Chaillu

Paul Belloni du Chaillu (circa 1831-1903), American explorer, born in France, probably in Paris. He spent his youth in Gabon, French Equatorial Africa, with his father, a French trader. In 1852 he went to the United States and later became a naturalized citizen. He led an expedition to central Africa in 1855 and returned to the U.S. four years later, bringing with him many previously unknown birds and animals, including the first gorillas ever seen in the U.S. His description of the expedition, Explorations and Adventures in Equatorial Africa (1861), aroused controversy, however, because it conflicted with prevailing geographical, zoological, and ethnological theories. Du Chaillu led a second expedition to Africa, confirming his first report and verifying rumours about Pygmy tribes in the forests of central Africa in *A Journey to Ashango-Land* (1867). After travelling (1871-74) in northern Europe, he wrote *The Land of the Midnight Sun* (1881).

## 22. Henry Morton Stanley

Sir Henry Morton Stanley 1841-1904, Anglo-American journalist, explorer, and empire builder, b. Denbigh, Wales. He grew up in poverty and came to America as a worker on a ship, which he jumped (1858) in New Orleans. Originally named John Rowlands, there he took a new name, which he claimed, apparently falsely, was that of his adoptive father. After fighting on both sides in the American Civil War and deserting, he drifted into journalism. His coverage of Lord Napier's Ethiopian campaign in 1868 for the New York Herald won him journalistic notice, and he later pursuaded the paper's editor to commission him to go to Africa to find David Livingstone . Stanley located the great explorer on Lake Tanganyika on Nov. 10, 1871. He claimed to have addressed him with the famous words, "Dr. Livingstone, I presume?," but probably did not actually do so. Failing to persuade Livingstone to leave Africa, Stanley returned to England with the news of his discovery. He found a mixed reception in England, where Livingstone's backers criticized Stanley's efforts and methods. Nevertheless, he succeeded in enhancing Livingstone's reputation and soon led a second expedition (1874-77), sponsored by newspapers, to further Livingstone's explorations. He followed the Congo River from its source to the sea, but he found the British uninterested in developing the region.

Stanley then accepted the invitation of Leopold II of Belgium to head another expedition. During this third journey (1879-84) he helped to organize the notorious Congo Free State, largely by persuading local chiefs to grant sovereignty over their land to the Belgian king. At the Berlin Conference he was instrumental in obtaining American support for Leopold's Congo venture. His last African journey (1887-89), to find Emin Pasha, helped to put Uganda into the British sphere of influence. A naturalized U.S. citizen, Stanley again became a British subject in 1892, sat in Parliament (1895-1900), and was knighted (1899). His spirited and often self-aggrandizing accounts of his adventures include *How I Found Livingstone* (1872), *Through the Dark Continent* (2 vol., 1878), *In Darkest Africa* (2 vol., 1890), and *The Exploration Diaries of H. M. Stanley* (ed. by R. Stanley and A. Neame, 1961). A British and American hero for about a century and certainly a man of great accomplishment, Stanley has fared rather poorly in recent histories, which have revealed instances of his lying about events in his life, duplicity in some of his dealings, and many acts of brutality toward Africans.

# 23. Dr. Frederick Albert Cook

Dr. Frederick Albert Cook was American explorer and Physician that is best known for his claim of being the first man that reached the North Pole in 1908. His claim is widely speculated to be false, and discovery was credited to the Robert Peary that reached the Northern Pole in 1909.

Frederick Cook was born on June 10, 1865 in Hortonville, Sullivan County, New York as a son of a recent German immigrant Dr. Theodore A. Koch and Magdalena Long. After receiving his M.D. status in 1890, he started his life as explorer. He was a member of a several Arctic expeditions, most notably with Robert Peary (1891-1892) and Adrien de Gerlache (1897–1899). During those missions, Cook also made acquaintance with famous Norwegian explorer Roald Amundsen.

His journey to the North Pole started in 1907 after his short exploration of the Mr. McKinley which brought him more controversy later on (he did not provide any proof that he reached its peak). Cook's North Pole expedition consisted of a very small team, only himself and two Inuit men (Ahpellah and Etukishook). After fourteen months on the Arctic, he returned to civilization on Greenland. Again, he did not manage to provide certain proof of him reaching the North Pole. According to his claims, he left Annoatok settlement in Northern Greenland in February 1908 and has reached Northern pole on April 22. From there they encountered several weather problems, molten ice that cut of his route, and has managed barely to survive reaching the Annoatok in spring of 1909. Logbooks with his measurements were never recovered and few pieces of sextant navigational data that Frederick Cook released in 1911 contained incorrect information.

In the following years, his reputation was severely damaged, and international press and scientist all claimed that expedition of Robert Peary was first on the Pole. During early 20s, he was incarcerated and sentenced to jail until 1930 for his unlawful involvement with Texas oil business.

He died on August 5, 1940 from the cause of cerebral hemorrhage.

## 24. Robert Peary

Robert Peary was an American explorer who is today best-known for his claim to be the first man who reached the North Pole in 1909. Although Frederick Cook reached Pole in 1908 lack of evidence made the international press and scientist to support Robert Pear's claim of success.

Robert Edwin Peary was born on 6 May 1850 in Cresson, Pennsylvania, USA. Between 1886 and 1891, he made first attempts of Arctic survival with two attempts to cross the frozen Greenland with dog sleds. During his time there, Peary studied the life of native Inuits and adopting their ways of life (hunting techniques, clothing and travel tactics). Even his wife Josephine joined him on several expeditions.

During early 1900s he had two journeys watch brought him some fame. First he explored northern regions of Greenland for which he received medals from American Geographical Society and Royal Geographical Society of London. In 1905, Peary embarked on a sea mission travelling with his ship Roosevelt through the icy sea between Greenland and Ellesmere Island reaching the sailed farthest north than any ship before him.

Peary's most successful mission started on the 6 July 1908 when he embarked from New York with the crew of 23 people. They reached Arctic on 1 March 1909 and majority of his crew remained at camp. Robert Peary and six more people continued toward the North and on 7 April 1909, he reached the Geographic North Pole. Sadly, when he returned to civilization he found out that Frederick Cook reached the pole a year earlier. However, he did not give up, and soon after American congress accepted him as the original "attainer" of pole. He was awarded with the position and pension of Rear Admiral, and he died ten year later in 1920.

To this day, there are several claims that he indeed did not reach North Pole. Some proof for that though lies in his navigation omissions and errors and as well as inconsistent reports of travel speeds.

# Famous
# Canadian Explorers

## 1. Pierre Le Moyne Iberville

Pierre Le Moyne Iberville (1661-1706), French-Canadian explorer and naval officer who fought against the British in Canada and founded the French colony of Louisiana. Iberville was born in what is now Montréal, Québec. Appointed a midshipman in the French navy at the age of 14, he was sent to France and served there until 1679, when he returned to Canada. After 1686 he led successive land and sea expeditions against stations of the Hudson's Bay Company in an effort to dislodge British power in Canada. After a victory over a superior British naval force, he captured Fort Nelson on Hudson Bay in 1697, thereby destroying the single remaining post of the Hudson's Bay Company in Canada.

In 1698 the French government commissioned Iberville to find and colonize the mouth of the Mississippi River. In 1699 Iberville became the first European to approach the Mississippi from its outlet at the Gulf of Mexico. He then explored the river as far north as the present-day city of Cairo, Illinois. On his return to the Gulf of Mexico, Iberville became the first European to sight Lake Pontchartrain, in what is now Louisiana. He named the lake for the count of Pontchartrain, then the head of the French navy. Also in 1699 Iberville, accompanied by his brother Jean-Baptiste Le Moyne, Sieur de Bienville, established a settlement at what is now Ocean Springs, Mississippi. Iberville was made a captain in the French navy in 1702 and assumed command of the West Indian fleet in 1706.

## 2. Robert Abram Bartlett

Robert Abram Bartlett (1875-1946), Canadian-American explorer, born in Brigus, Conception Bay, Newfoundland, and educated at the Methodist College at St. John's and at the Halifax Academy. He accompanied the American explorer Robert E. Peary on an Arctic expedition in 1897 and 1898, and from 1905 to 1909 he commanded the Roosevelt on the voyages during which Peary may have arrived at the North Pole (This claim is being disputed). On the final dash he accompanied Peary on land as far north as the 88th parallel.

Bartlett became an American citizen in 1911. He was captain of the Karluk on the Canadian Arctic expedition of 1913 and 1914.

After his ship was crushed by ice near Wrangel Island, Bartlett crossed the ice to Siberia with one Inuit and led back a party that rescued 13 survivors. He headed other expeditions to the Arctic in 1917 and each year from 1925 to 1935.

## 3. Sir Alexander Mackenzie

Sir Alexander Mackenzie (1764-1820), Canadian explorer and fur trader, born in Stornoway, Lewis with Harris Island, Scotland. He immigrated (1774) with his family to New York City and in 1779 moved to Montréal, where he joined the fur-trading firm later known as the North West Company. In 1789 he set out from Fort Chipewyan on Lake Athabasca for his first journey of exploration in northwest Canada. He explored from Great Slave Lake to the Arctic Ocean by travelling on the great river that now bears his name. Four years later, on a second expedition, he ascended the Peace River, crossed the Rocky Mountains, followed the Fraser River and several tributaries, and then struck overland to the Pacific Ocean. Mackenzie was the first man to explore the North American continent north of Mexico on an overland journey. He published his journals of the expeditions in 1801. He was knighted a year later.

## 4. Peter Skene Ogden

Peter Skene Ogden (1794-1854), Canadian fur trader and explorer, who lived in the western United States, including the coastal region of Oregon, northern California, and the Snake

River area. As a fur trader for the Hudson's Bay Company, he was led to new territory in dealing with the Native Americans west of the Rockies. Ogden made the first approach to the Sierra Nevadas from the east, visiting Carson and Owens lakes in 1829. In 1847 Ogden rescued the survivors of the Marcus Whitman massacre, in which the members of the missionary's family and 12 members of his group were slain by Native Americans of the Cayuse tribe. Ogden, Utah, is named in his honour.

## 5. David Thompson

David Thompson (1770-1857), Canadian surveyor and explorer, born in London. At the age of 14 he became an apprentice of Hudson's Bay Company, and from 1797 to 1812 he worked with the North West Company, exploring northwest Canada and keeping detailed notes of his travels. He developed great skill in astronomical and geodetic observation. He crossed the Rocky Mountains in Canada and eventually explored the whole length of the Columbia River before reaching Montréal, where he completed (1812-14) invaluable maps of western Canada. From 1816 to 1826 he was one of the appointed surveyors along the boundary between the United States and Canada. Although his contribution to North American geography was of major importance, he received scant recognition during his lifetime and died impoverished and almost blind.

## 6. John McLoughlin

John McLoughlin (1784-1857), Canadian-American explorer and fur trader, born in Rivière-du-Loup, Québec. He became a physician and joined the North West Fur Company, which later merged with the Hudson's Bay Company. In 1824 he was made superintendent of the Columbia district of the Hudson's Bay Company, an area comprising the present-day states of Washington, Oregon, and Idaho as well as the province of British Columbia. He established his headquarters at Fort Vancouver (now Vancouver, Washington); organized new trading posts and kept peace among the indigenous peoples; and won control of the fur trade on the Pacific coast. Recognizing the agricultural possibilities of Oregon, he encouraged settlement of the region by French-Canadian farmers. He resigned from the Hudson's Bay Co. in 1846, moved to Oregon City, and became an American citizen.

## 7. Louis Joliet

Louis Joliet (1645-1700), French-Canadian explorer, who led an expedition to explore the upper Mississippi River with Jesuit missionary Jacques Marquette. He was born probably in Beaupré, near the city of Québec, and educated in a Jesuit seminary for the priesthood. He also studied briefly in France, but in 1668, upon his return to New France (France's North American colonial empire), he abandoned the church to become a trader among the indigenous peoples. In 1669 he met Jacques Marquette. In 1672 Joliet, already familiar with the region, was chosen to lead an expedition in search of the upper reaches of the Mississippi River. Father Marquette was named chaplain for the party. The expedition, joined by five woodsmen, left Saint Ignace (now in Michigan) on May 17, 1673. They crossed Lake Michigan, ascended the Fox River, and descended the Wisconsin River. On June 17, 1673, the expedition entered the Mississippi River. The party then followed the Mississippi southward to a point below the mouth of the Arkansas River before turning back. Marquette remained at Lake Michigan while Joliet continued on to Québec, reaching it in 1674. On the return portion of the voyage Joliet lost his records in a canoe accident, but he replaced them from memory. Later Joliet explored in the region of Labrador and Hudson Bay. In 1697 he was appointed royal hydrographer of New France.

# Famous Danish Explorers

# 1. Vitus Jonassen Bering

Vitus Bering (1680-1741), Danish navigator. Vitus Jonassen Bering was born in Horsens, Denmark. He entered the newly formed navy of the Russian tsar Peter the Great and in 1724 was appointed to conduct an expedition to explore the water routes between Siberia and North America. Having taken supplies across the continent, Bering sailed from Kamchatka Peninsula in 1728. He passed north through the Bering Strait into the Arctic Ocean, but because of bad weather he did not sight the North American continent; he did prove, however, that the Asian and North American continents are not joined. Returning to Saint Petersburg in 1730, he sought another expedition to explore northeastern Siberia.

In 1733 Bering assumed command of a much larger and more ambitious undertaking, which eventually was responsible for the mapping of large areas of the northern Siberian coast. In June 1741 Bering set sail from Petropavl (which he had founded the previous year) for the North American continent. He sailed into the Gulf of Alaska and sighted the continent north of what is now Cape Saint Elias, Alaska, on July 29, and shortly afterward landed on Kayak Island. During the return voyage Bering and most of his crew were ill with scurvy, and his ship, encountering storms and fog, was wrecked on an uninhabited island, subsequently named Bering Island in his honour. Bering died there of exposure one month later, but a few survivors built a vessel in which they returned to Kamchatka in 1742.

# Famous German Explorers

# 1. Alexander von Humboldt

Alexander von Humboldt (1769-1859), German naturalist and explorer, best known for his many valuable contributions to the study of geophysics, meteorology, and oceanography.

Friedrich Wilhelm Heinrich Alexander, Freiherr von Humboldt, was born in Berlin on September 14, 1769, and educated privately and at various universities and the mining academy at Freiberg. Although he was known as a naturalist, diplomat, astronomer, mineralogist, and anatomist, his fame also rests on his exploration of Latin America. In 1799 he sailed from Spain, stopped briefly at the Canary Islands, and finally landed at Cumaná, Venezuela. Humboldt explored the entire length of the Orinoco River and most of the Amazon River system. He also travelled in Cuba, the Magdalena River basin of Colombia, and the Andes Mountains of Ecuador, where he ascended the volcano Chimborazo to an altitude of more than 5800 m (19,000 ft) above sea level. He studied ocean currents, relative temperature according to altitude, and magnetic intensity in relation to the equator, as well as minerals and plant and animal life. He spent the final period of his five-year exploration of America in Mexico. In 1804 he returned to Europe, and in 1829 he made a voyage of scientific exploration through the Ural and Altay Mountains of Russia. During the final years of his long life Humboldt wrote a five-volume work, Kosmos (The Cosmos, 1845-1862), in which he set forth not only his own vast scientific knowledge but also most of the accumulated scientific knowledge of geography and geology of the time. Kosmos has been called the first textbook of geophysics. Humboldt died in Berlin on May 6, 1859.

## 2. Heinrich Barth

Heinrich Barth (1821-1865), German explorer of Africa. After an education at the University of Berlin, Barth travelled (1845-1847) in modern Libya and Tunisia. In 1850 he joined a British-sponsored expedition, led by James Richardson, into the interior of West Africa. From Tripoli the group crossed the Sahara and reached Lake Chad, where Richardson then died. Taking command, Barth moved westward, exploring the middle section of the Niger River and discovering the upper reaches of the Benue River, a tributary of the Niger. He then pushed on (1852-1853) to Tombouctou (Timbuktu). Finally, he returned to Tripoli and then to London in 1855. Barth's five-volume *Travels and Discoveries in North and Central Africa* (1857-1858) contains information on, and maps of, many little-known regions.

## 3. Mehmed Emin Pasha

Mehmed Emin Pasha (1840-1892), German explorer and administrator in Sudan, in northeast Africa, who made important contributions to the study of the geography, natural history, and ethnography of northeastern Africa. Originally named Eduard Schnitzer, he was born in Opole, in what is now Poland, to German parents and studied medicine at the University of Berlin. From 1865 to 1875 he served as quarantine medical officer for the Ottoman Empire in Montenegro and Albania, and adopted the Turkish name Mehmed Emin. In 1875 he journeyed to Cairo, Egypt, where he was appointed medical officer in the Egyptian army under the British general Charles George Gordon. In this period he became known as Emin Effendi. In 1878 Gordon named him governor of Equatoria province in southern Sudan, with the title of bey. In that capacity Emin explored widely in southern Sudan and the surrounding regions, studying plant and animal life as well as the cultural characteristics of the African peoples he encountered.

In 1883 a popular revolt broke out in Sudan under the Islamic leader Muhammad Ahmad, known as the Mahdi. Emin, who had been promoted to pasha (viceroy), eventually found himself isolated by the Mahdi's forces north of Lake Albert, in what is now northern Uganda. In April 1888 he was rescued and resupplied by an expedition led by the Anglo-American explorer Henry Morton Stanley. Emin reluctantly agreed to evacuate the region with Stanley in 1889, and together they trekked southeast to Bagamoyo on the Indian Ocean coast. The next year he was commissioned by the German East Africa Company to lead an expedition into central Africa. He was killed by Arab slave traders in 1892 near Stanley Falls, in what is now northeastern Democratic Republic of the Congo.

# Famous Scottish Explorers

## 1. Joseph Thomson

Joseph Thomson (1858-95), Scottish explorer, who explored many parts of East Africa previously unseen by Europeans and filled his journals with valuable and detailed geographical information. He came upon (1879) Lake Rukwa (in modern Tanzania) and blazed a trail, unarmed, through the hostile Masai country between Zanzibar and present-day Uganda in 1882. Thomson explored (1885) modern northern

Nigeria and joined (1890) Cecil Rhodes's British South Africa Company, negotiating mining and trade agreements in what is now Zambia.

## 2. James Bruce

James Bruce (1730-1794), Scottish explorer, the first to follow the course of the Blue Nile to its confluence with the White Nile. He was born in Stirling County, Scotland, and educated at the University of Edinburgh. After a short business career he was appointed (1763) consul in Algiers, where he studied Oriental languages and medicine. In 1765 Bruce resigned his position and explored Roman ruins in North Africa. He continued his archaeological investigations in Rhodes, Cyprus, and Syria, examining various ruins, notably those of Baalbek (now in Lebanon) and Palmyra in Syria.

In his next important undertaking Bruce sought to discover the source of the Nile. In November 1770, after spending two years in Abyssinia (now Ethiopia), he reached the source of the Blue Nile, which he mistakenly considered to be of greater historical importance than the White Nile. Bruce claimed that he was the first to discover the source of the Blue Nile; it is known, however, that the Spanish Jesuit missionary Father Pedro Paez discovered it about 1615. Overcoming many difficulties and hardships, Bruce proceeded overland in 1771, following the course of the Blue Nile to its confluence with the White Nile, a journey that he was the first to accomplish. He wrote *Travels to Discover the Sources of the Nile*, in the years 1768-73 (5 volumes, 1790).

# 3. David Livingstone

David Livingstone, 1813-73, Scottish missionary and explorer in Africa, the first European to cross the African continent. From 1841 to 1852, while a medical missionary for the London Missionary Society in what is now Botswana, he crossed the Kalahari desert and reached (1849) Lake Ngami. He discovered the Zambezi River in 1851. Hoping to abolish the slave trade by opening Africa to Christian commerce and missionary stations, he travelled (1853) to Luanda on the west coast. Following the Zambezi River, he discovered and named Victoria Falls (1855) and reached the east coast at Quelimane, Portuguese East Africa (now Mozambique), in 1856. His *Missionary Travels* (1857) in South Africa is an account of that journey. Appointed British consul at Quelimane, he was given command of an expedition (1857-63) to explore the Zambezi region.

Livingstone returned to England (1864) and with his brother Charles wrote *The Zambezi and Its Tributaries* (1865). In 1866 he returned to Africa to seek the source of the Nile. He discovered lakes Mweru and Bangweula and in 1871 reached the Lualaba tributary of the Congo River. Sickness compelled his return to Ujiji on Lake Tanganyika, where the journalist H. M. Stanley found him in 1871. Unable to persuade Livingstone to leave, Stanley joined him on a journey (1871-72) to the north end of Lake Tanganyika. In 1873 Livingstone died in the village of Chief Chitambo. African followers carried his body to the coast; it was sent to England and buried in Westminster Abbey. Livingstone's last journals were edited by Horace Waller (1874).

## 4. Mungo Park

Mungo Park (1771-1806), Scottish explorer, born in Foulshiels, Selkirk. In 1795 he went to Africa to explore the Niger River. Upon arriving in present-day Gambia, he went 322 km (200 mi) up the Gambia to the trading station of Pisania (now Karantaba) and then travelled east into unexplored territory. He was captured by a local chief but escaped and in 1796 reached the Niger River at the town of Ségou. He travelled 129 km (80 mi) downstream as far as Silla before his supplies were exhausted. After his return to Great Britain in 1797, Park published an account of his trip in *Travels in the Interior of Africa* (1799). In 1805 he returned to Africa to explore the Niger, from Ségou to the mouth of the river, by canoe. His expedition was attacked at Bussa, however, and Park was drowned. An account of Park's second journey, taken from his journals, was published posthumously in London in 1815.

## 5. Hugh Clapperton

Hugh Clapperton (1788-1827), Scottish explorer whose account of the region now known as northern Nigeria was the first by a European. Born in Annan, Scotland, he went to sea at the age of 13 and later became a lieutenant in the Royal Navy. In 1821 the British Colonial Office sent him, along with explorers Walter Oudney and Dixon Denham, on the Bornu Mission to trace the true course of the Niger River in Africa. They crossed the Sahara from Tripoli, in present-day

Libya, and became the first Europeans to see Lake Chad, which Denham set off to explore on his own. From there, Clapperton and Oudney headed west into present-day Nigeria toward Kano but Oudney died along the way and Clapperton reached it alone. He then travelled on to Sokoto but, detained by local rulers, was unable to find a guide to take him the 240 km (150 mi) to the Niger. He returned briefly to England before coming back to West Africa in 1825. With British explorer Richard Lemon Lander, Clapperton travelled inland from the Bight of Benin to the Niger at Bussa and then to Sokoto. Again he was unable to find a guide, this time to help him reach Tombouctou far upstream (in what is now Mali). After more than a year at Sokoto, Clapperton became ill, reportedly with dysentery, and died in 1827. In an 1830 expedition, Lander succeeded in determining the true course of the Niger, proving Clapperton's theory that it flowed into the Gulf of Guinea. Clapperton's Narrative of Travels and Discoveries in Northern and Central Africa in the Years 1822-1823, and 1824 was published in 1828. His second expedition was recounted both in his own Journal (1829) and in Lander's Records of Captain Clapperton's Last Expedition to Africa (1830).